D1294049

THE RAINTREE ILLUSTRATED SCIENCE ENCYCLOPEDIA

VOLUME 2

ART-BRA

RAINTREE STECK-VAUGHN
L I B R A R Y
A Division of Steck-Vaughn Company

Managing Editors

Corinn Codye
Writer and editor of social science
    and science textbooks
Paul Q. Fuqua
Writer and editor of films, filmstrips,
    and books on scientific subjects

Raintree Editorial

Barbara J. Behm, Editor
Elizabeth Kaplan, Editor
Lynn M. Marcinkowski, Project Editor
Judith Smart, Editor-in-Chief

Raintree Art/Production

Suzanne Beck, Art Director
Kathleen A. Hartnett, Designer
Carole Kramer, Designer
Eileen Rickey, Typesetter
Andrew Rupniewski, Production Manager

Copyright © 1991 Steck-Vaughn Company

Text copyright © 1991, Raintree Publishers Limited Partnership

For photographic credits, see Volume 18

Drawn art copyright © 1991, 1984, 1979 Macdonald Children's
Books (A Division of Simon & Schuster Young Books) and Raintree
Publishers Limited Partnership

Library of Congress Number: 90-40559

Library of Congress Cataloging-in-Publication Data

The Raintree illustrated science encyclopedia.
    Includes bibliographical references and index.

    Summary: Presents principles, concepts, and people in the various fields of
science and technology.
    1. Science—Encyclopedias, Juvenile.   2. Technology—
Encyclopedias, Juvenile.   [1. Science—Encyclopedias.   2. Technology—
Encyclopedias.   3. Encyclopedias and dictionaries.]   I. Raintree Publishers.
Q121.R34   1991   90-40559
503—dc20   CIP
ISBN 0-8172-3800-X (set)   AC
ISBN 0-8172-3802-6 (Volume 2)

Cover photo: See page 122.
Title page photo: See page 201.

3   4   5   6   7   8   9   10   95   94   93   92

USING THE RAINTREE ILLUSTRATED SCIENCE ENCYCLOPEDIA

You are living in a world in which science, technology, and nature are very important. You see something about science almost every day. It might be on television, in the newspaper, in a book at school, or some other place. Often, you want more information about what you see. *The Raintree Illustrated Science Encyclopedia* will help you find what you want to know. The Raintree encyclopedia has information on many science subjects. You may want to find out about mathematics, biology, agriculture, the environment, computers, or space exploration, for example. They are all in *The Raintree Illustrated Science Encyclopedia*. There are many, many other subjects covered as well.

There are eighteen volumes in the encyclopedia. The articles, which are called entries, are in alphabetical order through the first seventeen volumes. On the spine of each volume, below the volume number, are some letters. The letters above the line are the first three letters of the first entry in that volume. The letters below the line are the first three letters of the last entry in that volume. In Volume 1, for example, you see that the first entry begins with **aar** and that the last entry begins with **art**. Using the letters makes it easy to find the volume you need.

In Volume 18, there are interesting projects that you can do on your own. The projects are fun to do, and they illustrate important science principles. Also in Volume 18, there are two special features—an index and a bibliography.

Main Entries. The titles of the main entries in *The Raintree Illustrated Science Encyclopedia* are printed in capital letters. They look like this: **CAMERA**. At the beginning of most entries, you will see a phonetic pronunciation of the entry title. In the front of each volume, there is a pronunciation key. Use it the same way you use your dictionary's pronunciation key.

At the end of each entry, there are two sets of initials. They often look like this: P.Q.F./J.E.P. The first set belongs to the person or persons who wrote the entry. The second set belongs to the special consultant or consultants who checked the entry for accuracy. Pages iii and iv in Volume 1 give you the names of all these people.

Cross-References. Sometimes, a subject has two names. The Raintree encyclopedia usually puts the information under the more common name. However, in case you look up the less common name, there will be a cross-reference to tell you where to find the information. Suppose you wanted to look up something about the metric temperature scale. This scale is usually called the Celsius Scale. Sometimes, however, it is called the Centigrade Scale. The Raintree encyclopedia has the entry **CELSIUS SCALE**. If you looked up Centigrade Scale, you would find this: **CENTIGRADE SCALE** *See* CELSIUS SCALE. This kind of cross-reference tells you where to find the information you need.

There is another kind of cross-reference in the Raintree encyclopedia. It looks like this: *See* CLOUD. Or it looks like this: *See also* ELECTRICITY. These cross-references tell you where to find other helpful information on the subject you are reading about.

Projects. At the beginning of some entries, you will see this symbol: **PROJECT** It tells you that there is a project related to that entry in Volume 18.

Illustrations. There are thousands of photographs, graphs, diagrams, and tables in the Raintree encyclopedia. They will help you better understand the entries you read. Captions describe the illustrations. Many of the illustrations also have labels that point out important parts.

Index. The index lists every main entry by volume and page number. Many subjects that are not main entries are also listed in the index.

Bibliography. In Volume 18, there is also a bibliography for students. The books in this list are on a variety of topics and can supplement what you have learned in the Raintree encyclopedia.

The Raintree Illustrated Science Encyclopedia was designed especially for you, the young reader. It is a source of knowledge for the world of science, technology, and nature. Enjoy it.

PRONUNCIATION KEY

Each symbol has the same sound as the darker letters in the sample words.

ə	balloon, ago	i	rip, ill	sh	shoot, machine
ər	learn, further	ī	side, sky	t	to, stand
a	map, have	j	join, germ	th	thin, death
ā	day, made	k	king, ask	t̲h	then, this
ä	father, car	l	let, cool	ü	pool, lose
au̇	now, loud	m	man, same	u̇	put, book
b	ball, rib	n	no, turn	v	view, give
ch	choose, nature	ng	bring, long	w	wood, glowing
d	did, add	ō	cone, know	y	yes, year
e	bell, get	ȯ	all, saw	z	zero, raise
ē	sweet, easy	ȯi	boy, boil	zh	leisure, vision
f	fan, soft	p	part, scrap	'	strong accent
g	good, big	r	root, tire	'	weak accent
h	hurt, ahead	s	so, press		

GUIDE TO MEASUREMENT ABBREVIATIONS

All measurements in *The Raintree Illustrated Science Encyclopedia* are given in both the customary, or English, system and the metric system [in brackets like these]. Following are the abbreviations used for various units of measure.

Customary Units of Measure

mi. = miles	cu. yd. = cubic yards
m.p.h. = miles per hour	cu. ft. = cubic feet
yd. = yards	cu. in. = cubic inches
ft. = feet	gal. = gallons
in. = inches	pt. = pints
sq. mi. = square miles	qt. = quarts
sq. yd. = square yards	lb. = pounds
sq. ft. = square feet	oz. = ounces
sq. in. = square inches	fl. oz. = fluid ounces
cu. mi. = cubic miles	°F. = degrees Fahrenheit

Metric Units of Measure

km = kilometers	cu. km = cubic kilometers
kph = kilometers per hour	cu. m = cubic meters
m = meters	cu. cm = cubic centimeters
cm = centimeters	ml = milliliters
mm = millimeters	kg = kilograms
sq. km = square kilometers	g = grams
sq. m = square meters	mg = milligrams
sq. cm = square centimeters	°C = degrees Celsius

For information on how to convert customary measurements to metric measurements, see the **METRIC SYSTEM** article in Volume 10.

ARTHROPODA (är′thrə päd′ə) Arthropoda is the largest phylum of the animal kingdom. It contains about 80 percent of all the known animal species in the world. Insects, shrimp, spiders, and crabs all belong to Arthropoda.

All arthropods have jointed legs. (*See* JOINT.) *Arthropoda* comes from the Greek words meaning "jointed foot." Arthropods also have segmented bodies. Most species have a head, thorax, and abdomen. Arthropods do not have bones, but they do have a skeleton on the outside of their bodies. This is called an exoskeleton. It is made up of a hard material called chitin. The covering of a lobster or a cricket is an example of a chitin exoskeleton. The exoskeleton is also called the cuticle. (*See* CHITIN; SKELETON.)

Because the exoskeleton is hard and cannot expand, it prevents the animal from growing larger. Arthropods have developed a special way to grow. They shed their exoskeleton from time to time and form another, larger one. When an animal grows too large for the new exoskeleton, it will shed the exoskeleton and grow another. This process is called molting. (*See* MOLTING.)

The arthropods are the most highly evolved invertebrate animals. They probably had two common ancestors with the annelids. (*See* ANNELIDA; INVERTEBRATE.) Arthropods have

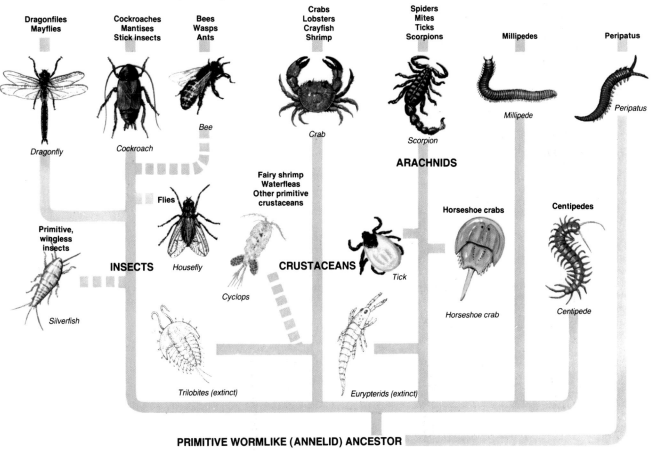

Arthropods are widespread and varied in structure. This "family tree" presents the main groups of arthropods. Two extinct forms, the trilobites and the eurypterids, lived more than 400 million years ago. A living fossil arthropod is the horseshoe crab, which is not actually a crab but an arachnid. The horseshoe crab has lived almost unchanged for 160 million years. The peripatus resembles the annelid worms, from which it evolved.

the most complex nervous system of the invertebrates. They have antennae that are used for touching, smelling, and hearing. Many arthropods have compound eyes. One large eye is made up of hundreds of tiny eyes, each of which forms a separate image.

The Arthropoda phylum is divided into several classes. (*See* CLASSIFICATION OF LIVING ORGANISMS.) The major classes are Insecta (insects), Crustacea (crustaceans), Arachnida (spiders), Chilopoda (centipedes), and Diplopoda (millipedes). *See also* ARACHNID; CENTIPEDE; CRUSTACEAN; INSECT; MILLIPEDE.

S.R.G./C.S.H.

ARTICHOKE (ärt′ə chōk′) Artichokes are plants belonging to the composite family. (*See* COMPOSITE FAMILY.) There are two kinds of plants called artichokes—the globe artichoke and the Jerusalem artichoke. The globe artichoke is native to the Mediterranean region. It is grown commercially in California. Its edi-

Globe artichokes are vegetable plants that have edible buds.

ble, unopened flower heads, or bud clusters, grow on stalks that are about 2 to 3 ft. [60 to 90 cm] high. The globe artichoke looks like a thistle. The Jerusalem artichoke is closely related to the sunflower. Its edible tubers, or swollen underground stems, look like potatoes. The Jerusalem artichoke grows to a height of 5 to 12 ft. [1.5 to 3.7 m].

G.M.B./F.W.S.

ARTIFICIAL INSEMINATION *See* BREEDING.

ARTIFICIAL INTELLIGENCE (ärt′ə-fish′əl in tel′ə jens) Artificial intelligence can be created by designing and programming a machine, especially a computer, so that it "thinks" and "reasons" like humans. Scientists working on artificial intelligence have developed computers and other machines to solve problems. Also, these computers "remember" their past mistakes and do not make them again. They get better at solving problems by learning from experience.

Artificial intelligence has been used in many fields. In medicine, computers have been programmed with information about many kinds of illnesses. Doctors can then diagnose a patient for those illnesses. In industry, computer-driven robots are used to assemble parts. Computers can also translate languages and even become expert chess players. *See also* COMPUTER.

P.Q.F./L.W.

ARUM FAMILY The arum (ar′əm) family consists of about a thousand herbaceous plants, most of which are tropical. They are monocotyledons. (*See* HERBACEOUS PLANT; MONOCOTYLEDON.) Their leaves are shaped like swords. Most members of the arum family have brightly colored spathes (flowerlike parts) that are easily mistaken for flowers. Most of the species wind around or onto other plants. (*See* EPIPHYTE.) Some varieties found in swampy areas of North America include skunk cabbage, jack-in-the-pulpit, and elephant's ear.

Some of these plants give off a strong odor that attracts flies and other insects. The insect is then trapped by the spathes and the leaves. The movement of the insect trying to escape pollinates the plant. (*See* POLLINATION.)

One kind of arum plant is the jack-in-the-pulpit. The tiny flowers grow on a spike called a spadix, which is enfolded in a flowerlike hood called a spathe. Most species of arum are poisonous, but the roots may be made edible by cooking.

Most plants in the arum family are poisonous. The poison can be removed by cooking. The light starchy paste left after boiling the roots is called arrowroot. It is used to thicken puddings and other desserts.

A.J.C./M.H.S.

ASBESTOS (as bes'təs) Asbestos is a nonmetallic mineral, which may be separated into fibers. Chrysotile, the most widely used kind of asbestos, is found mainly in Canada and the Soviet Union. (*See* MINERAL.)

Asbestos mineral fibers can be spun to make thread. This thread is woven into fabrics that, being made from rock, are very resistant to heat and chemicals and are good electrical insulators. Asbestos suits are worn to fight large, very hot fires, and asbestos fabrics have been used in theater curtains.

Asbestos was once used as insulation and in ceiling panels in schools and other public buildings throughout the United States. However, during the 1980s, much of the asbestos insulation and ceiling panels were removed because microscopic fibers in asbestos were thought to cause cancer. This practice is controversial because of the high costs associated with the removal of the asbestos. Nonetheless, governmental health agencies consider asbestos to be a hazardous waste capable of causing both cancer and lung disease. Strict public health laws are now in effect regarding its use, handling, and removal from buildings.

J.J.A.; C.C./R.H.; E.W.L.; L.W.

ASCHELMINTHES (ask hel'min thēz) The phylum Aschelminthes includes class Nematoda (roundworms); class Rotifera (rotifers), and everal other lesser-known animals. (*See* ANIMAL KINGDOM; WORM.) The roundworms are very common animals. They are found in almost every kind of environment around the world. One acre [0.4 hectare] may contain as many as 2.4 billion roundworms. Many roundworms are parasites. (*See* PARASITE.) Some are found in people. One worm that is a parasite in people can grow up to 3.3 ft. [1 m] in length. People get the worms by accidentally swallowing their eggs. Some roundworms are passed from dogs to humans.

Rotifers are one of the most common kinds of animal found in fresh water. (*See* ROTIFER.) Most rotifers are microscopic, rarely growing larger than 0.02 in. [0.5 mm]. They are important food for fishes and other aquatic species.

S.R.G./C.S.H.

ASCORBIC ACID *See* VITAMIN.

ASEPSIS (ā sep′səs) Asepsis is the complete absence of any disease-causing microorganisms, commonly called germs. It is important for hospitals to provide an aseptic environment because microorganisms can enter cuts or wounds and cause infections. To ensure asepsis, disease-producing microorganisms are killed by sterilization. (*See* STERILIZATION.)

Operating rooms, surgical instruments, and other equipment are sterilized with steam, dry heat, or boiling water. The doctors and nurses wash with special antiseptics and wear sterile gowns and face masks. The patient's skin is cleaned with an antiseptic before surgery. (*See* ANTISEPTIC.)

Aseptic technique has replaced the simple, less effective antiseptic methods used in the past. Asepsis has resulted in fewer infections after operations. *See also* MICROORGANISM.

A.J.C./L.V.C.; J.J.F.

PROJECT

ASEXUAL REPRODUCTION (ā sek′shü əl rē′prə dək′shən) Most organisms produce offspring by mating with a member of the opposite sex. (*See* REPRODUCTION.) Sometimes offspring can be produced without the help of a member of the other sex. This is called asexual reproduction. There are many different types of asexual reproduction.

One-celled organisms, such as amebas, reproduce by binary fission. The original ameba simply splits in two. Before the split occurs, however, the ameba must split every part inside so that there are two of everything in the cell. When the cell splits, each half gets one of each part, so that the new amebas are identical.

Another type of asexual reproduction is budding. In many lower animals, such as the cnidarians, a new animal grows off of the side of another one. Then it breaks off and becomes a separate animal. (*See* BUDDING.)

Every effort is made in hospitals to keep operating rooms free from microorganisms that can enter cuts or wounds and cause infections.

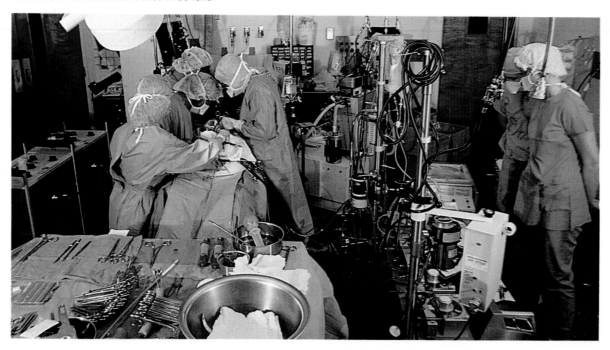

Members of phylum Platyhelminthes can reproduce by regeneration. If a worm of this phylum breaks in half, each half grows back the missing piece. After a while, there are two whole worms.

In parthenogenesis, eggs are laid without being fertilized by a male. (*See* FERTILIZATION; PARTHENOGENESIS.) The offspring are identical to the mother.

Some lower plants produce spores asexually. Spores are similar to seeds, except that they are not produced by a female plant. They are produced by a plant without a sex. The spore may grow into a male or female plant, which can engage in sexual reproduction and produce a plant that will again produce spores. (*See* ALTERNATION OF GENERATIONS; SPORE.)

Some of the higher plants, such as trees, can also reproduce asexually. If a branch of a willow tree breaks off and lands in water or moist soil, it can form roots and grow into another tree. This process is called vegetative propagation. (*See* VEGETATIVE PROPAGATION.)

All of the offspring produced by asexual reproduction are just like their parents. They are called clones. (*See* CLONE.) The more common sexual reproduction allows for change between parent and offspring. This change makes it possible for living things to adapt successfully to changing conditions. If organisms reproduced only asexually, evolution would be nearly impossible. *See also* ADAPTATION; EVOLUTION. S.R.G./E.R.L.

ASH Ash trees are hardwood, deciduous trees that grow in North America, Europe, and Asia. (*See* DECIDUOUS TREE.) They belong to the genus *Fraxinus*. They are members of the olive family. Sixteen species are native to the United States. The most common of these are the white ash, red ash, and black ash.

Leaves and a seed cluster from a red ash tree are pictured.

Ash trees may grow to be more than 100 ft. [30 m] tall. Because ash is a strong hardwood, it is used in making baseball bats, oars, and the handles of shovels. A.J.C./M.H.S.

ASPARAGUS (ə spar′ə gəs) Asparagus is the name given to about 150 species of plants. Asparagus, naturally grown anywhere from Siberia to southern Africa, is a member of the Liliaceae, or lily, family. Asparagus plants stand by themselves or can climb onto objects, such as fences or posts. Their roots give rise to unusual leaves, which look like small scales. Asparagus plants have small, greenish yellow flowers in the spring, followed by small red berries in the fall.

Asparagus can be grown in many kinds of soil. The best type of soil in which to grow asparagus year after year is a loose and light clay with a great deal of organic matter. Asparagus thrives in soil too salty for most crops. It does not grow well in soil containing large amounts of acid.

Three kinds of asparagus are sold as vegetables. Green spears and green spears with white stalks are the kinds produced for the fresh market. Asparagus is a good source of vitamin A.

A few types of asparagus, such as the *Asparagus plumosus*, are prized for their delicate leaves. They are used in corsages and in other plant arrangements. 　　　J.J.A./F.W.S.; L.O.S.

ASPARTAME (as′pər′tām) Aspartame is a synthetic, or humanmade, food sweetener. Aspartame is many times sweeter than sugar, so a lesser amount is used. This results in fewer calories than if sugar were used to sweeten food. Aspartame has many uses. For example, aspartame is used in diet soft drinks and as a sugar substitute in coffee and tea. Aspartame largely replaced saccharine and other artificial sweeteners that were believed to cause cancer. Aspartame is sold under the trade names *NutraSweet* and *Equal. See also* SUGAR. 　　　P.Q.F./J.E.P.

ASPHALT (as′fôlt′) Asphalt is a black or brown mineral material used in making roads and in waterproofing roofs, water tanks, and boats. It is also used as an adhesive. Asphalt consists of hydrocarbons combined with nitrogen, sulfur, and oxygen. (*See* HYDROCARBON.) It can be obtained from natural deposits, called asphaltum, or from the distillation of crude petroleum. (*See* DISTILLATION.) Large deposits of natural asphalt occur in Texas, Oklahoma, Utah, and California. The world's largest deposits are found in western Canada. Venezuela and Iran also have asphalt deposits.

Asphalt becomes a heavy liquid when heated. To make road surfaces, the hot liquid is mixed with crushed stone. The mixture is then spread and rolled.

Asphalt is an ancient building material, used by the Babylonians and mentioned in the Bible. It was used to seal the walls of a reservoir in Pakistan in 3,000 B.C. 　　　W.R.P./J.M.

ASPIRIN (as′pə rən) Aspirin, or acetylsalicylic acid, is a white, powdered analgesic. An analgesic is a substance that reduces or stops pain without causing unconsciousness or complete loss of feeling. Besides being an analgesic, aspirin reduces inflammation and fever. It is used to treat symptoms of arthritis, colds, and influenza (flu), as well as headaches and other body pains. Aspirin also has been found effective in keeping clots from forming in the blood. Some research suggests that aspirin may be useful in preventing strokes. (*See* STROKE.) Aspirin is mildly acidic and may irritate some people's stomachs. Manufacturers often add sodium bicarbonate, a form of salt, to make aspirin less acidic. Doctors may also recommend acetaminophen, a less irritating analgesic. Aspirin usually is sold in the form of pills or caplets. *See also* ANALGESIC.
　　　P.W./J.E.P.

ASS The ass is a relative of the horse. It looks like a zebra without stripes. Its height to the top of its shoulder is 3 to 5 ft. [90 to 150 cm]. It can run very swiftly. It has long ears and is usually gray with a dark brown or black mane.

Wild asses live on the hot, dry plains of Africa and Asia. The onager is a wild ass of Africa. The kulan, the kiang, and the ghorkhar are wild asses of Asia. Because they are hunted for their hides and their meat, wild asses are in danger of becoming extinct.

The African wild ass is the ancestor of the donkey. Thousands of years ago, humans captured the wild asses of Africa. By training these animals to do work, people developed a domesticated animal that was given the name *donkey.* Today, there are many varieties of donkeys. *See also* DONKEY.
　　　G.M.B./J.J.M.

ASSAYING (as′ā ing) In science, assaying is a method used to find out how much and what kinds of metals are in a rock or an unknown alloy. (*See* ALLOY.) At one time, assaying was concerned only with finding out how much gold or silver was in an alloy.

Assays are carried out by using various means of chemical analysis. The main methods of assaying are the wet process and the dry process. In the wet process, the unknown sample is mixed with other chemicals in solution. (*See* SOLUTION AND SOLUBILITY.) The resulting products are separated and weighed. During the dry process, the sample may be crushed and pure substances sifted out. The sample may also be roasted and its products collected and measured.   J.J.A./A.D.

ASTATINE *See* ELEMENT.

ASTER (as′tər) The aster is a flowering perennial plant of the composite family. There are more than two hundred known varieties in North America. The flower of this herbaceous plant is shaped like a disk. (*See* COMPOSITE FAMILY; HERBACEOUS PLANT; PERENNIAL PLANT.) It has many thin, pointed petals, which give it a starlike appearance. Its colors range from white to pink to deep blue and purple.

The aster blooms in late summer. In some warmer areas, the flowers may last until early winter. Although some asters may grow from seeds, reproduction is usually by vegetative propagation. (*See* VEGETATIVE PROPAGATION.) Relatives of the aster include the chrysanthemum and the sunflower.   A.J.C./M.H.S.

There are more than two hundred varieties of asters in North America. Their many-petaled, disk-shaped flowers range in color from white to deep purple.

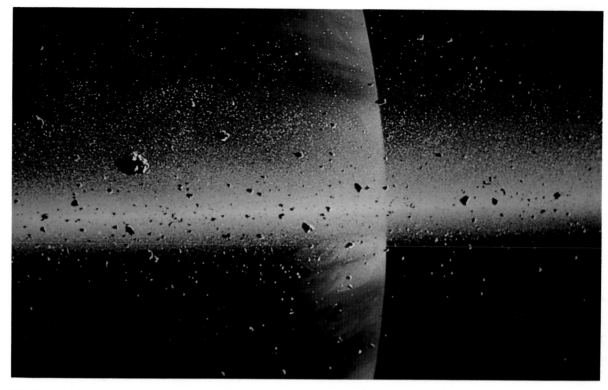

This drawing shows part of the asteroid belt, with Jupiter in the background.

ASTEROID (as′tə ròid′) An asteroid is a minor planet that orbits the sun. Most asteroids travel in space between the orbits of Mars and Jupiter in a region known as the asteroid belt. Asteroids are much smaller than major planets. Some asteroids are only about 1 mi. [1.5 km] in diameter. Ceres, the largest asteroid, has a diameter of 490 mi. [784 km]. It is nearly spherical in shape. There are about 100,000 asteroids. The majority of them are too small to be seen from earth. Ceres is the only one that can be seen without a telescope.

Eros is a small asteroid that wanders from the asteroid belt and comes closer to the earth, within 16 million mi. [25.6 million km], than any of the others. Scientists observe the movement of Eros to determine the astronomical unit, the distance between the earth and the sun. *See also* ASTRONOMICAL UNIT.

W.R.P./E.W.L.; D.H.M.; C.R.

ASTHMA (az′mə) Asthma is a very common disease that causes a person to feel short of breath or to have other problems with breathing. When a person with asthma, called an asthmatic, has an asthma attack, he or she may have difficulty breathing, causing him or her to gasp and wheeze. A feeling of tightness in the chest and a chronic (long lasting or recurring) cough also may be signs of asthma. Asthma attacks often occur at night, after heavy exercise, after prolonged exposure to cold air or irritating fumes, or when a person is emotionally upset. A viral infection of the nose and throat also may trigger an asthma attack.

In an asthma attack, the bronchial tubes of the lungs narrow. (*See* LUNG.) This may occur because of a tightening of the muscles around the bronchial tubes or because of a swelling of the membranes that line the tubes and increased production of mucus by these membranes. The flow of air through the tubes is then partially blocked, resulting in the symptoms described above. Asthma is commonly caused by allergy to dust, pollen, animal fur, or certain foods. Asthma is often linked with hay fever, another kind of allergy. (*See* ALLERGY.)

A doctor identifies asthma by doing a physical exam. He or she may use tests of lung function, a chest X ray, allergy skin tests, or blood tests to determine which substances a person is allergic to and what the best treatment of the disease is. Treatment depends on the severity of the symptoms. During a severe asthma attack, the patient must go to a hospital emergency room, where he or she may be given oxygen and drugs to control the symptoms. For less severe asthma, the doctor may prescribe any of various drugs in the form of an aerosol inhaler, which the patient uses during waking hours to keep the bronchial tubes wide open. Patients with very severe asthma may need to take drugs called steroids daily.

J.J.A./L.V.C.; J.J.F.; M.H.M.

ASTROLABE (as′trə lāb′) An astrolabe is an instrument that was used by ancient Greek ship navigators and astronomers. It measured the altitude, or height, of stars and planets above the horizon in degrees, minutes, and seconds. (*See* MEASUREMENT.) Ship captains used this information to navigate their ships. Today, sea navigators use an instrument called a sextant to obtain the altitudes of heavenly bodies. The sextant is a highly improved version of the astrolabe. *See also* NAVIGATION; QUADRANT.   W.R.P./J.VP.

ASTROLOGY (ə sträl′ə jē) Astrology is an unscientific approach to predicting what will happen in a person's life by studying the moon, the sun, the planets, and the stars. Astrology is based on a belief that these heavenly bodies influence human affairs. Astrology is also based on the belief that a person will have particular characteristics depending on what position the heavenly bodies were in when he or she was born.

Astrology began more than three thousand years ago in Babylonia. It was the beginning of the science of astronomy, which is the scientific study of the heavenly bodies, including their motions, size, and composition. (*See* ASTRONOMY.) The astrology of ancient Egypt identified twelve signs of the zodiac that are named after constellations. People who practice astrology use the zodiac in their predictions. These people are called astrologers. Even though most scientists believe modern astrology has no scientific basis, many people still believe in it. *See also* CONSTELLATION; ZODIAC.   G.M.B./E.W.L.; D.H.M.; C.R.

ASTRONAUTICS (as′trə nȯt′iks) Astronautics is the science of flight in space beyond the earth's atmosphere. It applies knowledge gained from various sciences to the design, construction, and operation of spacecraft. Astronautics deals with ways to control and track the flight of spacecraft. It also deals with the unusual conditions (such as weightlessness) that crews experience during flight outside the earth's gravity. (*See* GRAVITY; WEIGHTLESSNESS.)

Astronautics is a relatively recent science. It had its beginnings in the science of aeronautics, which deals with flight within the earth's atmosphere. Because vehicles designed for spaceflight also have to be able to operate within the earth's atmosphere (during launch and reentry), astronautics and aeronautics are

Satellites (top) help scientists study weather patterns. Satellites also serve communications, military, and navigational purposes. Space shuttles are moved from place to place by attaching them to large aircraft (bottom left). John Glenn was the first American to orbit earth (bottom right).

overlapping sciences. (*See* AERONAUTICS.) Astronautics deals mainly with ways to use jet propulsion to control the direction and speed of a spacecraft when it is largely free of the earth's gravitational pull. (*See* JET PROPULSION.)

The first recorded use of the word *astronautics* was in 1927. The development of a distinct science of spaceflight occurred rapidly after the Soviet Union launched the first two *Sputnik* satellites in 1957. In July 1969, the United States successfully sent two astronauts, in the spacecraft *Apollo 11*, to the moon. By 1975, more than a hundred space missions had been successfully flown, including seven moon landings. (*See* APOLLO PROJ-

ECT.) The first reusable manned spacecraft—the space shuttle *Columbia*—was successfully tested by the United States in 1981. Many space shuttle flights have been made since then.

As astronautics rapidly became a fully developed science, the purposes of each new spaceflight became more ambitious. Spacecraft have been fitted with many kinds of instruments for gathering information about the environment of space. All of the moon's surface has been mapped in great detail by both manned and unmanned spacecraft. Television cameras in unmanned spacecraft have taken closeup pictures of Mars, Jupiter, and other planets in our solar system. Various kinds of scientific detectors mounted on space probes have sent back to earth information about such things as weather, temperature, and biological conditions. These probes can be controlled by radio. Their flight path can be changed, their cameras aimed, and their equipment turned on and off.

Astronautics has developed satellites whose purposes include military reconnaissance, long-distance communications, radiation measurement, and astronomical observation. Some of these satellites remain in constant orbit. Navigation satellites send radio signals that can help a ship at sea check its course. Communications satellites make it possible to send live television pictures over very long distances. (*See* SATELLITE.)

Astronautics has provided much new information for astronomers. Satellites can take photographs of the sun and planets without the distortion that occurs when the photographs are taken from earth. Unmanned satellites equipped with scientific detectors can obtain information that cannot yet be obtained by manned spacecraft.

Astronautics will eventually make it possible to establish a base on the moon, orbit a permanent space station, and even send an expedition to Mars. *See also* SPACE TRAVEL.

P.G.Z./G.D.B.

ASTRONOMICAL UNIT The astronomical (as′trə näm′i kəl) unit is used by astronomers and astrophysicists to measure distances in outer space. It is approximately equal to 93,000,000 mi. [149,600,000 km], the mean distance between the earth and the sun. *See also* LIGHT-YEAR; PARSEC.

G.M.B./J.VP.

ASTRONOMY (ə strän′ə mē) Astronomy is the scientific study of the stars, planets, and other things that make up the universe. Scientists who work in the field of astronomy are called astronomers. They study celestial (heavenly) bodies with telescopes, radar, spectroscopes, cameras, artificial satellites, and spacecraft. Astronomers gather information about everything outside of the earth's atmosphere. They also provide information for navigation and for the measurement of time on earth.

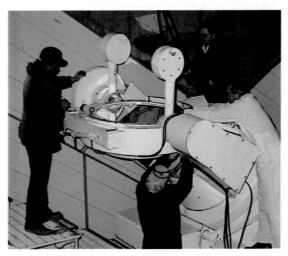

This mirror is used in the solar telescope at Kitt Peak in Arizona. Solar telescopes allow astronomers to study the closest star, our sun, in detail.

Scientists believe that this ancient building in Mexico was a kind of observatory from which Mayan priests studied the stars and planets (top). Many scientists think that this pictograph from a canyon wall in Arizona represents a supernova, or exploding star (bottom). They believe that the supernova was observed by American Indians living in the area hundreds of years ago.

Ancient roots of astronomy Astronomy is thousands of years old. It has its roots in astrology, the unscientific study of heavenly bodies. (*See* ASTROLOGY.) In ancient Babylonia, the sun, the moon, and the stars were studied to establish a measurement of time. In ancient Egypt, when certain stars appeared at certain locations, the people knew that it was time for the Nile River to flood. For example, the appearance of the constellation Aquarius was a warning. It meant that preparations for the flood should begin. (*See* CONSTELLATION; ZODIAC.) In North and South America, the Mayan and Incan civilizations based their architecture on astrological observations.

Astronomy began in ancient Greece. About 2,600 years ago, Pythagoras guessed that the earth was a sphere at the center of the universe. About 800 years later, another Greek scholar, Ptolemy, wrote a book that was to be the basis of astronomy for the next 1,400 years. The mistake made by almost all of the early astronomers was to think that the earth was at the center of the universe. They thought that the sun, moon, stars, and planets revolved around earth, which did not move at all.

Beginnings of modern astronomy Modern astronomy began with the work of Nicolaus Copernicus, in the 1500s. (*See* COPERNICUS.) In 1543, he established that the earth moved around the sun. Copernicus explained that all planets orbited the sun, correcting Ptolemy's idea of the universe. Later, Tycho Brahe, of Denmark, spent many years studying the stars and the planets. (*See* BRAHE, TYCHO.) He kept careful records of the positions of the stars and planets. Brahe died before he was able to complete his work. Another astronomer, Johannes Kepler, used Brahe's work to discover how planets moved around the sun. (*See* KEPLER, JOHANNES.) Kepler was a mathematician. He was able to show that each planet traveled in an elliptical, or oval-shaped, orbit around the sun.

Galileo and Newton At the same time that Kepler was calculating the orbits of the planets, Galileo was developing the telescope. (*See* GALILEO; TELESCOPE.) This instrument enabled humans to see the sky better than ever before. In 1610, Galileo observed the moons of Jupiter and the moonlike phases of Venus. After Galileo 's death, in 1642, the English astronomer and mathematician Sir Isaac Newton made the most important discovery since the time of Copernicus. (*See* NEWTON, SIR ISAAC.) Newton's three laws of gravitation explained the movements of all heavenly bodies. He proved, for example, that gravitation controls the orbit of the moon. Newton also invented the spectroscope, which was to become a valuable tool for astronomers. (*See* SPECTROSCOPE.)

Discovery of the planets Using the discoveries of Copernicus, Brahe, Kepler, Newton, and others, astronomers later located planets that had never before been found. In 1781, Sir William Herschel discovered Uranus. (*See* HERSCHEL, SIR WILLIAM FREDERIC.) Neptune was discovered by J. G. Galle in 1846. Early in the 1900s, Sir Percival Lowell predicted the existence of Pluto. (*See* LOWELL, PERCIVAL.) In 1930, the planet was sighted by astronomers by Lowell Observatory in Flagstaff, Arizona. The discovery of Pluto established the nine principal planets of the solar system. Five of the nine planets had been known since ancient times. (*See* PLANET; SOLAR SYSTEM.) Ceres was the first asteroid (minor planet) to be discovered. It was found by astronomers in 1801. By the middle of the 1900s, astronomers had identified about 1,600 asteroids. Scientists continue to find them. (*See* ASTEROID.)

Stars While some astronomers searched for planets, other astronomers searched for stars. In the early 1800s, Joseph Fraunhofer became one of the first astronomers to use Newton's spectroscope to examine starlight. His work led to a new branch of astronomy called astrophysics. (*See* ASTROPHYSICS.)

Photography Photography is an important tool of astronomy. In 1840, astronomers first photographed the moon. By 1850, photographs of the stars had become possible. Today, astronomers use cameras that are very complex and sensitive. These cameras are able to photograph stars that cannot be seen by the eye, even with a telescope. In the United States, astronomers at Harvard University have been adding information to a catalog of stars since 1885. It is called the *Henry Draper Catalogue.* It contains photographs and measurements of more than 400,000 stars.

Meteorites, meteoroids, and comets Astronomers also study meteorites, meteoroids, and comets. Meteoroids are meteorites that have landed on the earth. Some weigh more than a ton. In Arizona, there is a crater 4,000 ft. [1,210 m] across and 600 ft. [183 m] deep that was caused by the impact of a meteor. Comets may also strike the earth. (*See* COMET; METEOR.)

Complex electronic tools allow scientists to observe the heavens in many different ways. This picture, for example, shows a color-enhanced image of a galaxy, or large cluster of stars. Created with a computer, the picture shows the different energy levels in the galaxy as different colors.

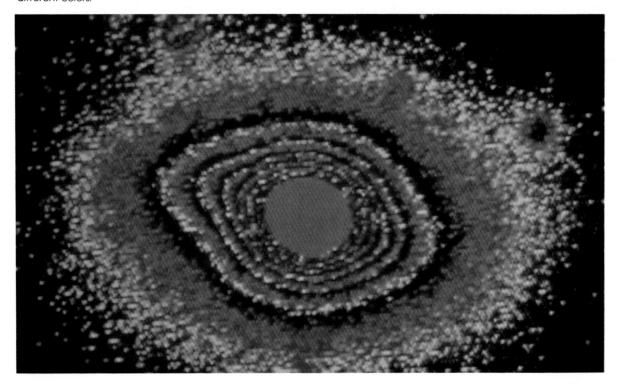

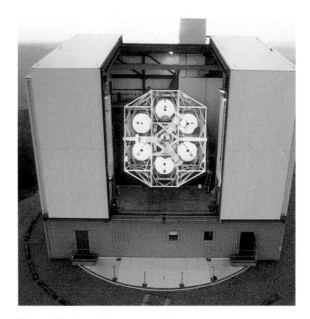

The multi-mirror telescope on Mt. Hopkins in Arizona is one of the world's most advanced telescopes. Instead of the one large mirror used in most telescopes, this instrument uses six smaller mirrors to gather and focus light from distant stars.

Telescopes Telescopes are the instruments most often used by astronomers. With one of the largest reflecting telescopes in the world, astronomers at the Palomar Observatory in California are able to photograph stars that are a billion light-years away. The world's largest refracting telescope is at Yerkes Observatory in Wisconsin. Radio telescopes are used to receive and record radio waves that are sent out by objects in space. In the 1960s, astronomers discovered new kinds of objects in space by using radio astronomy. (*See* PULSAR; QUASAR.) In 1965, astronomers used radar to learn how long it takes for Mercury and Venus to rotate (spin). (*See* RADIO ASTRONOMY.)

Recent developments The space technology of the twentieth century has led to great advances in astronomy. One of the most important advances has been the regular use of space probes and artificial satellites. (*See*

SATELLITE; SPACE TRAVEL.) In 1947, the United States launched a rocket to take the first photographs outside the atmosphere. In 1959, a Soviet space probe televised the first pictures of the side of the moon that is always turned away from earth. In the 1960s, astronauts left astronomical equipment on the moon, and space probes landed on Venus and Mars. During the *Skylab* missions of the 1970s, the cloud-covered surface of Venus

The Pioneer X space probe, launched by the United States in early 1972, was the first probe to reach Jupiter. This picture is an artist's interpretation of how the craft looked as it passed the moon after leaving earth.

was mapped in great detail. The *Voyager* spacecrafts sent back spectacular photos of Jupiter and its moons (1979), Saturn (1980-1981), Uranus (1986), and Neptune (1989) as the probes flew by each planet. Several probes were launched by different nations in 1985 to view Halley's comet in early 1986. The *Magellan* space probe was launched in 1989. It went into orbit around Venus in 1990 and photographed the planet's surface. This provided the first complete map of the surface of Venus.   G.M.B.; C.C./D.H.M.; C.R.

ASTROPHYSICS (as'trə fiz'iks) Astrophysics deals with the physical and chemical makeup of celestial, or heavenly, bodies. It

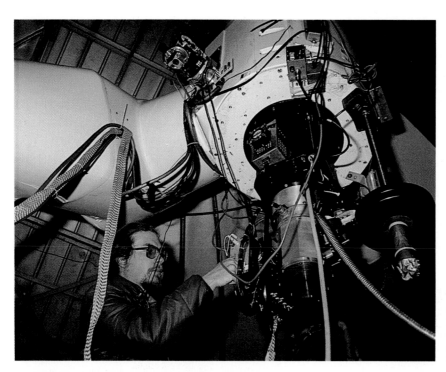

This telescope is equipped with devices that convert light from the stars into electronic signals. The signals are recorded on magnetic tape for later analysis by astrophysicists.

applies the theories and methods of physics to determine the structure of stars and to solve other problems in astronomy. (*See* PHYSICS.)

Astrophysics is primarily an observational science. It includes the study of the kinds of energy given off by the sun and the other stars, as well as by planets and nebulae (large clouds of gases and dust). In particular, it is the study of the light and electromagnetic radiation given off by the bodies. (*See* ELECTROMAGNETIC RADIATION.)

By analyzing the light coming from a star, an astrophysicist can determine what physical elements are present in the body of the star. This analysis is made with a spectroscope, which converts the light waves given off by a star into the various colors they contain. The density and range of the colors in the spectrum are part of the evidence the astrophysicist uses. (*See* SPECTROSCOPE.)

Most stars give off radio waves and X rays. Astrophysics uses techniques of radio astronomy and X-ray astronomy. Evidence gained by study of magnetic fields, light waves, radio waves, and X rays given off by stars has allowed astronomers to calculate such things as a star's mass, temperature, and inner structure. (*See* RADIO ASTRONOMY; X RAYS.)

Astrophysics also deals with distances between stars and with the motion of stars, as well as that of planets and their satellites. It helps astronomers make maps of galaxies. The instruments used for this purpose include telescopes, photoelectric cells, radio antennas, and computers. (*See* TELESCOPE.)

Space exploration has greatly increased the amount of information available to astronomers. For example, telescopes and other astrophysical instruments carried outside the earth's atmosphere by balloons and satellites have enabled astronomers to view the sun's atmosphere and surface clearly. (*See* SATELLITE.)

Instruments carried by satellites have greatly increased the ability of astronomers to collect information. They have also led to the discovery of unusual astronomical bodies—black holes, pulsars, and quasars—whose natures are being closely studied. (*See* BLACK HOLE; PULSAR; QUASAR.) Astrophysicists are giving close attention to quasars, for instance, because quasars are the most distant stars or galaxies visible from the earth. A quasar is faint blue in color when viewed through a telescope. Study of the light of quasars indicates that they are moving away from the earth's galaxy (the Milky Way) at nearly the speed of light. (*See* RED SHIFT.) The brightness of a quasar has been calculated as more than that of one hundred galaxies combined.

What is intriguing to astronomers is the fact that light reaching the earth from quasars was emitted billions of years ago. One of the difficulties in studying very distant heavenly bodies is that only evidence that existed in the past can be observed. Scientists cannot directly determine anything about the present reality of even the closest stars to earth's galaxy. That is because their light—which is where scientists get evidence about them—takes so long to reach earth. Light from the sun, for example, takes about eight minutes to reach the earth. However, light from distant stars may take millions of years to reach the earth.

The light emitted by a star can give the astrophysicist information about its surface. However, what the inside of a star is like must be inferred, using the sciences of physics and chemistry. For example, if the surface temperature of a star is 5,000 degrees, the inside temperature will be millions of degrees. By taking into account a star's weight, mass, surface temperature, and light, an astrophysicist can calculate its approximate age and may even be able to trace its probable history. *See also* ASTRONOMY; COSMOLOGY; GALAXY; SOLAR SYSTEM.   P.G.Z./G.D.B.

ATHEROSCLEROSIS *See* ARTERIOSCLEROSIS.

ATHLETE'S FOOT *See* FUNGUS.

ATMOSPHERE (at′mə sfir) The atmosphere is the mass of gases that surrounds the earth. It is about 500 mi. [800 km] high. Its total weight is almost 6 million billion tons [5.5 million billion metric tons.]

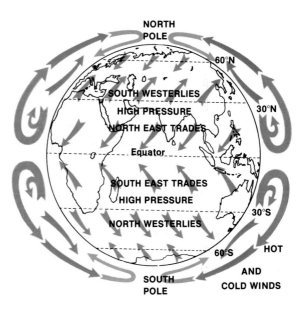

Wind belts form in the atmosphere when hot air rises from the equator, and cold air from the poles moves in.

The force of gravity holds the earth's atmosphere around the earth. Other planets in our solar system also have a gravitational force strong enough to hold an atmosphere in place. (*See* GRAVITY.) However, their atmospheres are different from the one that surrounds earth. Earth's atmosphere is made up of dust, gases, and water vapor. Two of its gases, nitrogen and oxygen, make up 99 percent of the volume of air. Air is necessary to life. Scientists are concerned about the effects of air pollution because of the limited supply of air available to us. (*See* AIR.)

The atmosphere protects the earth from harm. It prevents too many ultraviolet rays from reaching the earth by acting as a filter between the earth and the sun. Acting as a blanket, the atmosphere keeps the earth from losing too much heat at night. It also protects the earth from most meteorites and cosmic rays. (*See* COSMIC RAYS; METEOR.)

The atmosphere changes as it gets higher and farther away from earth. The higher it goes, the thinner it gets, because the molecules of its gases are farther apart. The air is so thin above 25,000 ft. [7,500 m] that travelers must have extra oxygen to survive.

To help describe the differences among the levels of the atmosphere, scientists have divided it into four layers. Starting with the layer next to the earth's surface, they are the troposphere, the stratosphere, the ionosphere, and the exosphere.

Troposphere About 75 percent of the entire mass of the atmosphere is in the troposphere. It starts at the earth's surface and extends outward to an altitude (height) of 5 to 10 mi. [8 to 16 km]. It is the layer in which all of the earth's weather occurs.

The troposphere is about 80 percent nitrogen and about 20 percent oxygen, with small amounts of carbon dioxide. Most of the water and dust in the atmosphere is to be found in this layer.

About 45 percent of the sun's radiation falling on earth is absorbed by the ground; 18 percent is absorbed by the atmosphere; and 37 percent is reflected back into space. Most of the 18 percent absorbed by the atmosphere is absorbed by the carbon dioxide, water vapor, and dust in the troposphere. The carbon dioxide, water vapor, and dust are thicker near the ground. This is why the warmest tempera-

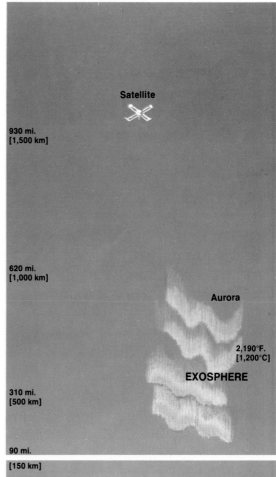

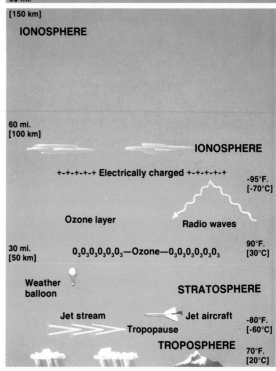

A cross section of the earth's atmosphere shows the main layers and their average temperatures. There are no clear-cut boundaries between the layers of the atmosphere.

tures in the troposphere are to be found near the earth. As the height of the troposphere increases, its temperature drops at the rate of 20°F. per mi. [7°C per km].

In the upper troposphere, unusual winds are found. These are narrow and fast-moving currents of air called jet streams. (*See* JET STREAM.) In and beyond the upper troposphere, the atmosphere contains too little oxygen to support life.

The uppermost limit of the troposphere is called the tropopause. Its altitude varies from 5 mi. [8 km] in some places to 11 mi. [18 km]. Its temperature also varies, from -60°F. [-51°C] at the lowest altitudes to -110°F. [-79°C] at the highest.

Stratosphere The stratosphere begins 10 mi. [16 km] above the earth and extends out to a height of 50 mi. [80 km]. There are only a few clouds in the stratosphere. They are made up mostly of ice crystals. These crystals form on the small particles of dust that remain when meteors burn up in the atmosphere. The only winds in the stratosphere are jet streams and other fast-moving winds. Jet streams blow toward the east. Because they help planes fly faster and save fuel, pilots like to fly in them on long trips.

Jet pilots also prefer to fly in the stratosphere to avoid the storms that occur in the troposphere below. Airplanes flying in the stratosphere may leave behind trails like long, thin, white clouds. These are called *contrails,* which is short for "condensation trails." They are made up of freezing water from a plane's exhaust.

The upper stratosphere is warmer than the other layers of the stratosphere. This is because its ozone filters the energy of the ultraviolet light from the sun. Because it controls the amount of ultraviolet light that reaches the earth, the ozone layer is very important. Scientists are concerned about its possible pollution by the exhaust of supersonic jets and its destruction by chlorofluorocarbons used on earth. (*See* CHLOROFLUORCARBON; OZONE.)

Ionosphere The ionosphere begins at an altitude of 50 mi. [80 km] and ends about 300 mi. [480 km] above the earth. It is called the ionosphere because the sun's radiation ionizes most of the molecules of its thin air. (*See* IONS AND IONIZATION.) The ionosphere is important in radio astronomy and in communications with artificial satellites. It allows short, high-frequency waves to pass through. It is important in radio communications because it reflects low- and medium-frequency radio waves back to the ground.

Sometimes the ionosphere is disturbed by particles from the sun. These disturbances cause glowing lights in the sky called auroras. (*See* AURORA.)

Exosphere The exosphere is the outermost layer of the atmosphere. It begins 300 mi. [480 km] above the earth, but its boundary with outer space has not yet been clearly defined. The outer parts of the exosphere contain mostly hydrogen and helium gases. The exosphere has a high temperature because the few atoms and molecules in its very thin air are able to move about very rapidly.

Pressure and circulation of the atmosphere Look at the top of a desk. Imagine a column of air pressing on it that is about 500 mi. [800 km] high. The total amount of weight on the desk top is called atmospheric pressure. At sea level, the atmosphere has a pressure of 14.7 lb. per sq. in. [1.03 kg per sq. cm].

Formation of an atoll: A volcano rises above the level of the sea, forming an island. A reef of coral forms around the volcano (top left). As the volcano begins to settle beneath the waves, the coral reef builds up higher. The coral organisms can survive only near the surface (top right). Even though the volcano may become completely worn away, a circular atoll is left, enclosing a lagoon (bottom). Many such atolls may be found in the Pacific Ocean.

There are many forces that account for the circulation of the atmosphere. One force is a result of the sun warming the air near the equator more than it warms the air at the poles. The uneven temperatures make the atmosphere circulate, carrying air along the ground from colder to warmer regions.

In addition, atmospheric pressure varies from one region on earth to another. Air near the ground tends to flow from areas where pressure is higher to areas where it is lower. Circulation results when the differences in pressure even themselves out.

H.G./C.R.

ATMOSPHERE (UNIT) An atmosphere (at′mə sfir) is a unit of atmospheric pressure. It equals 14.7 lb. per sq. in. [1.03 kg per sq. cm]. That is the pressure produced by a column of mercury in an upright tube that is 30 in. [76 cm] high. An atmosphere is also equal to 1,013 millibars, and 101.325 newtons per square meter. Air has a pressure of approximately one atmosphere at sea level. *See also* BAROMETER; MILLIBAR; NEWTON.

W.R.P./R.W.L.

ATOLL (a′tȯl′) An atoll is a ring or horseshoe-shaped group of coral islands surrounding a body of seawater. Atolls are found in tropical seas, where corals grow best. (*See* CORAL.) The water must be shallow, with much sunlight upon it. Normally, the lower limit for coral growth is between 197 ft. [60 m] and 295 ft. [90 m]. A very unusual drilling at the Eniwetok Atoll in the Marshall Islands discovered at least 5,000 ft. [1,525 m] of coral.

There are a number of theories why coral can form to such a great depth. One suggestion is that sea levels have slowly risen, allowing coral to form in further layers. Another theory explains the formation of layers of coral as the result of the slow sinking of land beneath the seas.

J.J.A./W.R.S.

ATOM (at′əm) is the smallest part of an element having all the properties of that element. (*See* ELEMENT.) All matter (anything that has mass) is made up of atoms. It is difficult to realize how extremely small an atom is. For example, this page is more than a million atoms thick.

Atoms are made up of even smaller particles. Every atom consists of a central part called a nucleus. Electrons move around the nucleus. The nucleus is very small compared with the size of an atom. If the diameter of an atom were the size of a football field (100 yd. or 91.44 m), the nucleus would be the size of a pea. In this sense, an atom consists mostly of space. (*See* NUCLEUS, ATOMIC.)

The nucleus is made up of two basic kinds of particles: protons and neutrons. Their masses are almost equal, and they are both about 1,850 times heavier than an electron. This means that almost all the mass of an atom is concentrated in the nucleus. The mass of the nucleus is less than the mass of its protons and neutrons. This is because when the particles form a nucleus, some of their mass is converted to energy to hold them together. The neutrons have no electric charge, but both the protons and the electrons are charged. The proton is positively charged, and the electron has an equal negative charge. An atom has an equal number of protons and electrons. This makes the atom electrically neutral. (*See* ELECTRON; NEUTRON; PROTON.)

Electrons, protons, and neutrons are referred to as *subatomic particles*. Protons and neutrons are, in turn, made up of even smaller particles called quarks. (*See* QUARK.) The rest of this article focuses on protons, neutrons, and electrons.

Atoms of each different element are different. The difference between one kind of atom and another lies in the number of protons in the nucleus.

The number of electrons moving around the nucleus is the same as the number of protons inside it. Hydrogen has one proton in the nucleus and one electron outside it. Uranium has a nucleus containing 92 protons and therefore 92 electrons surrounding it. These electrons are flying around the nucleus at great speeds. Their arrangement is very complicated and it is difficult to know where any electron is at any moment. However, a simple way of thinking about them is to imagine them to be in orbit around the nucleus, like a spacecraft orbiting the earth or a planet orbiting the sun. These orbits are called shells. There are several different shells. The farther away the shell is from the nucleus, the more electrons it can hold. The shell closest to the nucleus can only hold two electrons. This shell may only have one electron, as it does in a hydrogen atom. When this shell has two electrons, as in helium, the shell is said to be filled. The second shell can hold up to eight electrons, the third up to eighteen, and so on. The electrons in an atom always arrange themselves so that the shells nearest the nucleus are filled first.

The outer electrons are responsible for the chemical properties of the atom. Atoms are most stable when their outer shells are filled. If they have an unfilled outer shell, they try to become more stable by forming collections of atoms called molecules. (*See* MOLECULE.) Some atoms, such as helium, do not have any unfilled shells. These atoms, therefore, do not form ordinary molecules. These elements

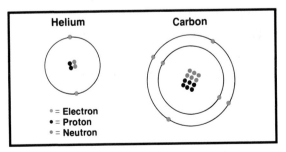

At left above is a model of a helium atom; at right above is a carbon atom. Both have their inner shell filled, with two electrons. The models are not done to scale; in reality, the nucleus is only about 1/1,000 of the total size of the atom.

occur in nature as single atoms. They are said to be monatomic. Atoms of some other elements, such as hydrogen, are joined together in pairs by bonds. Such molecules are said to be diatomic.

Sometimes an atom loses an electron. It then becomes positively charged. An atom can also gain an electron and become negatively charged. An atom that gains or loses an

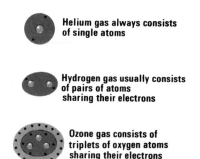

Helium gas always consists of single atoms

Hydrogen gas usually consists of pairs of atoms sharing their electrons

Ozone gas consists of triplets of oxygen atoms sharing their electrons

The drawings above show molecules that contain only one kind of atom. The atoms of helium occur singly. Helium is a monatomic gas.

electron is said to be ionized. The charged atom is called an ion. Since unlike charges attract each other, positive ions attract negative ions. When they come together, they form a chemical bond. This kind of bond is called an ionic or electrovalent bond. When atoms combine in this way, they both end up with completed outer shells. (*See* IONS AND IONIZATION; VALENCE.)

Atoms can also bind together by sharing electrons. The bond formed is called a covalent bond. The electrons spend part of the time with one atom and part of the time with the other. In this way, they can make the outer shells of both atoms full.

Isotopes Just as atoms can have different numbers of electrons and protons, they can also have different numbers of neutrons in the nucleus. Atoms having the same number of protons but a different number of neutrons from other atoms are still atoms of the same element. However, they are said to be isotopes of that element. For example, hydrogen exists in three different isotopes, called normal hydrogen, deuterium, and tritium. Normal hydrogen has one proton and no neutrons in its nucleus. Deuterium has one proton and one neutron in its nucleus. Tritium has one proton and two neutrons. (*See* ISOTOPE.)

Investigating the atom Atoms are too small to be seen in an optical microscope or an electron microscope. They can, however, be seen with a field ion microscope. The atoms appear only as patches of light with little shape. Scientists do not have to see atoms in order to learn about them. Chemists can discover how atoms react together by seeing

Isotopes are atoms of the same element that have different numbers of neutrons in the nucleus. The table shows details of isotopes of hydrogen. To identify each isotope, a symbol is used, with numerals indicating the number of particles in the nucleus as well as the number of electrons.

ISOTOPE	SYMBOL	PROTONS	NEUTRONS	ELECTRONS	ATOM
Hydrogen	1 H 1	1	0	1	
Deuterium	2 H 1	1	1	1	
Tritium	3 H 1	1	2	1	

how large samples of substances react together. Physicists can find out how atoms are arranged in crystal lattices. They do this by passing X rays through the crystals and studying the resulting pattern of X rays. (*See* CRYSTAL.) The spectrum of light produced in a spectroscope gives information on the arrangement of electrons inside an atom. (*See* SPECTROSCOPE.) Physicists can also research how atoms react when they are bombarded or collided, using three kinds of chambers: the bubble, cloud, and spark chambers. As the atoms pass through these chambers, they leave behind visible trails. Photographs are taken of the trails, which the physicists later study. (*See* ACCELERATORS, PARTICLE.)

The most recent atomic research involves the use of trapping devices to isolate, count, and study atoms. By the mid-1980s, physicists were able to trap a small group of sodium atoms, about 100,000, for one or two seconds. Larger traps now hold small groups of atoms for more than two minutes. Various trapping systems involve the use of magnetism, laser or polarized light, or systems to cool the atoms. (*See* LASER; MAGNETISM; POLARIZED LIGHT.) Multiphoton resonance ionization (MPRI) is another trapping device that allows scientists to count very small groups or even single atoms.

These trapping devices are used with cooling devices. Cooling devices are what actually slow the motion of the atoms. An atom would have no motion at all if it were cooled to -459.67°F. [-273.15°C], which is absolute zero. Scientists came close to achieving this temperature and stopping the motion of an atom in 1989. However, scientists still have not been able to actually reach absolute zero. By slowing atoms, scientists hope to build more precise atomic clocks and better satellite navigation systems and make new discoveries about atomic collisions. (*See* ABSOLUTE ZERO; CLOCK; NAVIGATION.)

Atomic energy Atomic energy is energy produced by the nucleus of an atom. For this reason, it is better called nuclear energy. This energy can be obtained by fission or by fusion. In fission, the nuclei (plural of *nucleus*) of large atoms split to form smaller nuclei. When they split, the nuclei lose some of their mass. The lost mass has been converted to energy. Fusion occurs when the nuclei of small atoms, such as hydrogen, join together, with a release of energy. *See also* FISSION; FUSION; NUCLEAR ENERGY; NUCLEAR PHYSICS.

C.C.; M.E./A.I.; E.W.L.; E.D.W.; L.W.

ATOMIC NUMBER An atomic (ə täm′ik) number is the number of protons in the nucleus of an atom. Since each proton in the nucleus has one positive electric charge, the total number of positive electric charges in the nucleus is equal to the atomic number. This number is the same as the number of electrons surrounding the nucleus of a neutral atom. Each of these electrons has one negative charge.

Every element has a different atomic number. This provides a way to identify any element. In the periodic table, the elements are arranged in order according to atomic number. *See also* ATOM; ELECTRON; ELEMENT; NUCLEUS, ATOMIC; PROTON.   J.J.A./A.D.

ATOMIC WEIGHT Atomic (ə täm′ik) weight is the weight, or mass, of one atom of an element compared with the weight of one atom of carbon-12. The atomic weight of an atom is found by adding the number of its protons (atomic number) and the number of its neutrons. Carbon-12 has 6 protons and 6 neutrons.

Scientists originally chose oxygen as the standard against which to measure atomic weights because oxygen is so common. However, because the element carbon combines readily with most other elements, it was chosen as the standard in 1960. Atomic weights of elements are not given as whole numbers. For instance, the atomic weight of carbon is 12.011. This figure represents the average weight of all carbon atoms, not the weight of a single atom. The weight is greater than 12 because it includes isotopes of carbon.

Atomic weight is also called mass number or mass unit. A neutron weighs about 1 mass unit. A mass unit is very small. It is equal to 1.660×10^{-24} grams, or .00000000000000000000000166 grams. Because a mass unit is so small, atomic weights are given as numbers that show a relative value. Relative value indicates that sulfur, with an atomic weight of 32, is twice as heavy as oxygen, which has an atomic weight of 16. *See also* ATOM; ATOMIC NUMBER; CARBON; ELEMENT; ISOTOPE; NEUTRON; PROTON.

R.H.H./J.M.

ATP ATP, adenosine triphosphate, is an important chemical substance that is usually formed in the mitochondria of living cells. (*See* KREBS CYCLE; MITOCHONDRIA.) ATP stores energy for use within the cells. When energy is needed for metabolic activities, such as nerve, gland, or muscle function in animals or the changing of glucose to form proteins, cellulose, or starch in plants, ATP supplies it. (*See* METABOLISM.)

ATP contains three phosphate molecules that are held together by energy-rich chemical bonds. When energy is required, one of these bonds breaks, releasing energy. One phosphate splits off, leaving ADP (adenosine diphosphate). This reaction (ATP → ADP + P + energy) is controlled by enzymes. (*See* ENZYME.)

The cells constantly renew their supplies of ATP. Animals form the energy-rich ATP by using energy released from digested food. (*See* RESPIRATION.) Plants renew their ATP supplies during photosynthesis by using energy from sunlight. (*See* PHOTOSYNTHESIS.) Although ATP is usually formed in the mitochondria, it is released for use by any part of the cell.

A.J.C./E.R.L.; M.H.M.

AUDIO RECORDING *See* SOUND RECORDING.

AUDUBON, JOHN JAMES (1785-1851) John James Audubon was one of the first American naturalists and ornithologists to study and paint birds of the United States. (*See* ORNITHOLOGY.) His drawings and paintings were of birds in their natural surroundings.

John James Audubon

Audubon painted some 1,055 life-sized pictures and had them published in London as *The Birds of America.* Original copies of this book are now very valuable. They are found mostly in large libraries and museums.

Audubon did much to publicize the value of wildlife. The National Audubon Society was named in his honor and is still one of the major wildlife societies in the United States.

P.G.C./D.G.F.

AUK (ôk) Auks are seabirds belonging to the family Alcidae. They have short wings, and their legs are set far back on their bodies. They are excellent swimmers and divers, using their wings as paddles and their feet as rudders. Auks are usually black and white. They spend the winters feeding on fish and plankton in the northern Atlantic and Pacific oceans. (*See* PLANKTON.) In the spring, huge colonies of auks come ashore, nesting in the cliffs. The female lays one or two eggs in cracks in the rocks. The parents stay with their young until they are well grown.

One species, the great auk (*Alca impennis*), became extinct in 1844. This bird could not fly. It was hunted ruthlessly for its feathers and meat. The existing twenty-one species of alcids are about one-third the size of the great auk and are able to fly. The little auk (*Plautus alle*), or dovekie, is about 8 in. [20 cm] long and feeds on plankton. Other small auks are called auklets or sea sparrows.

A.J.C./M.L.

AURORA (ə rōr′ə) An aurora is a natural display of light in the sky. Occasionally, the night sky in the northern hemisphere glows with bright green, red, blue, and yellow colors. This is called the aurora borealis. The aurora australis is the name for the same display that occurs in the southern hemisphere. The auroras are usually located near the north or south poles at heights of 50 to 100 mi. [80 to 160 km]. Some may be as high as 600 mi. [1,000 km].

When there is an increase in sunspot activity, the clouds of charged atomic particles that the sun sends out increase in strength. (*See* SOLAR WIND; SUNSPOT.) These particles travel through space in all directions. As they enter the earth's atmosphere, the magnetism at the poles changes the direction and speed of the particles. These particles then collide with air molecules in the cold, thin ionosphere, the

The display of colored lights in the sky known as the aurora borealis is produced when tiny charged particles from the sun collide with air molecules high in the atmosphere.

third layer of the atmosphere. This causes colored light. This process may continue for hours, often lighting the sky for an entire evening. *See also* MAGNETIC STORM.

A.J.C./C.R.

AUSTRALOID (ōs′trə lòid′) Australoid is the name given to a race of people found in Australia and Tasmania. Australoid people have dark skin and slender bodies. They have curly hair and large bushy eyebrows, large lower jaws, and large teeth.

In Australia, Australoid people are known as Aborigines. Before the Europeans came to Australia in the eighteenth century, there were probably thousands of different tribes of Aborigines. The way of life of the Europeans clashed with the ways of the Aborigines. Soon, fighting and killing became common. The Aborigines were no match for the weapons of the Europeans and were driven into the bush country, or outback.

In the 1920s, areas of land called reserves were set aside for the Aborigines. Now there are only a few thousand Aborigines living in the style of their ancestors. There are around 100,000 full-blooded Aborigines and those of mixed blood living in cities and small towns in Australia. The Australian Federal Office of Aboriginal Affairs has been established to protect the rights of the Aborigines.

There are no longer any Australoid people in Tasmania. They were all killed by Europeans in the eighteenth and nineteenth centuries. *See also* ABORIGINE.

A.J.C./S.O.

AUTOMATION (ôt′əmā′shən) Simply stated, automation is the use of machines to run other machines. It is a way of making a device, a process, or a system operate automatically. Human effort is not involved in the actual work. Once a person has planned what the machine should do and has turned on the power, the machine does the rest. Unlike workers whom they replace, such machines do not make mistakes, get tired, or take time off for sickness. However, they also cannot think for themselves or make judgments. They can only do what people have instructed them to do.

The word *automation* first came into general use around 1950. However, automation really began with the steam-operated textile machines of eighteenth-century England. The steam engines that powered those machines were fitted with automatic valves and devices that controlled their speed. In 1801, Joseph Marie Jacquard, a Frenchman, suggested the use of cards with a pattern of holes punched in them. He used the cards to automate a loom. Today, similar cards are used to control various kinds of automated machines. Early in the twentieth century, American industry used automated machines in the mass production of automobiles. Because machines often surpassed human workers in job performance, many other industries turned to automation.

Science and technology soon responded to the call of business and industry for faster and more efficient production. New scientific discoveries, especially in electronics, changed the modern world much as the inventions of the Industrial Revolution had done. Advances in radio, television, telecommunications, and aviation helped lay the groundwork for the dawning of the space age in the 1950s.

Space travel posed a new set of problems. Automation was the answer to many of them. How could human beings control something as fast as a rocket in flight? The need for instant access to information was vital. This need was met by computers, which can do high-speed calculations. The need for speedy, accurate, nonhuman performance was met by totally automated machines called robots. Computers and robots working together seem to have unlimited capacity for getting things done rapidly and efficiently. It is not surprising, then, that a race toward total automation has developed among the United States, Japan, and West Germany. Largely responsible for this forward leap of automation is the great progress made in computer science.

Computers are being used to control most automated industrial systems. Petroleum refineries, for example, are being run almost completely by computer. The few workers needed to operate the plant spend most of their time in a control room watching dials and other indicators. The computer sends and receives signals to and from various machine parts. It turns valves on and off automatically and detects and reports possible trouble spots. The memory of the computer has been programmed to do all this.

Many other large plants are operated in this way—for example, textile mills, steel mills, and automobile and aircraft plants. Advanced computer systems control the equipment of the banking industry and many other large businesses. Also, because computers can perform at rates that may be as high as millions of operations per second, their use with the equipment of scientific and technological laboratories is invaluable. Automated libraries quickly provide such research facilities with information essential to their work. *See also* COMPUTER; ROBOTICS.

H.S.B./G.D.B.; F.J.M.

The need in industry for the efficient performance of repetitive tasks has been met by completely automated machines called robots. The robot pictured is assembling vacuum cleaners.

Early automobile manufacturers, such as the Ford Motor Company, were pioneers in the development of mass production. Workers in an early Ford plant are pictured in the historic photograph at left.

AUTOMOBILE (ŏt′ə mō bēl′) An automobile, or car, is a four-wheeled, self-propelled passenger vehicle. A gasoline, diesel, or electric engine provides the force that moves an automobile. The smallest automobiles carry two people: the driver and the passenger. The largest autos can carry ten or more people. Automobiles are produced in large, automated factories that build many vehicles each day. (*See* AUTOMATION.) The largest automobile plants in the United States are near Detroit, Michigan.

History In 1769, Nicolas Cugnot of France used a steam engine to propel a crude wheeled vehicle. The first practical internal combustion engine was built by a French inventor, Etienne Lenoir, about 1860. (*See* ENGINE.) A German engineer, Nikolaus Otto, built a more efficient gasoline engine in 1862. In 1885, Karl Benz and Gottlieb Daimler, of Germany, used Otto's engine on four-wheeled carriages to make the first true automobiles. (*See* BENZ, KARL.) Early models were built slowly by hand and were expensive. In 1913, Henry

Ford, an American, introduced the conveyor belt to carry automobile parts on assembly lines. (*See* CONVEYOR; FORD, HENRY.) This made it possible to produce many automobiles in a short time. Ford was able to lower his prices so that many more people could afford to own automobiles. Other manufacturers did the same.

There were several major United States automobile manufacturers in the 1920s. Of them, only three are still in business: Ford Motor Company, General Motors, and Chrysler.

After World War II (1939-1945), Volkswagen, a German company, began to sell many of its small cars in the United States. They were called Beetles. Today, cars produced in Germany, Japan, and other countries account for a large number of all automobile sales in the United States.

Assembly An automobile body is attached to a structure of steel beams called a chassis. The chassis is very strong. It absorbs many strains and stresses. The body consists of thin sheet

There are many steps involved in the design and manufacture of today's automobiles. Designers often start with pencil sketches of their ideas (above). The designs are refined and, eventually, full-size clay models are made (bottom). Workers put the finishing touches on seats before they are installed in the cars (left).

Robots perform 95 percent of the welding tasks in modern automobile assembly plants.

metal with some structural steel beams built in for added strength. Some bodies are made of aluminum or fiberglass.

Automobiles are built on assembly lines. Groups of workers—or, increasingly, robots—install different parts as the uncompleted automobiles are moved past them. Major units, such as engines and transmissions, are assembled on their own assembly lines. When completed, they are brought to the main assembly line and put into the automobile at the proper time. Computers are used to keep track of all the hundreds of parts that go into each car. Completed automobiles are rolled off the end of the assembly line, tested, and delivered to dealers by trains and large trucks.

Engines The gasoline engine is used as the power source in most automobiles. Some autos are powered by diesel engines. (*See* DIE-

SEL.) Diesel engines are heavier and more expensive than gasoline engines. They last longer than gasoline engines, however. Electric engines that run on stored electricity in batteries have been developed for small cars to be used for city driving. They are not in wide use. Some manufacturers have experimented with gas turbine engines for automobiles. However, they are too expensive to produce in quantity. (*See* TURBINE.)

Most automobile engines have four, six, or eight cylinders. Gasoline is mixed with air and compressed (squeezed) inside each cylinder. It is ignited with a spark from a spark plug. The explosion forces a piston to move downwards. An arm attached to the piston turns a large shaft at the bottom of the engine called the crankshaft.

Most engines are mounted in the front end of the automobile. Front-mounted engines drive the front wheels rather than the rear wheels in most new automobiles. Some engines are mounted in the rear of the car and drive the rear wheels.

An automobile engine needs electricity to ignite the gas-air mixture in its cylinders. It generates its own electricity with one of two kinds of machines: a generator or an alternator. Some of the electricity is stored in a lead-acid battery. Every car has a battery. Electricity from the battery is used to start the engine and to operate lights and accessories. (*See* BATTERY; GENERATOR, ELECTRICAL.)

Engines create a great amount of heat when they are running. The explosions in the cylinders have a temperature of 3,500°F. [1,927°C]. Cylinder temperatures must be brought down to about 160°F. [71°C] in order to prevent damage to the engine. Cool air is blown across the engine by a fan attached to the front end. In some engines, a cooling system circulates a mixture of water and chemicals around the cylinder walls to cool them. The water-chemical mixture gets hot in the process. It is cooled again by running it through the radiator mounted in front of the engine. Other engines are air cooled.

Lubrication systems circulate oil throughout the engine to reduce friction between moving parts. Exhaust systems remove waste gases that result from combustion in the cylinders. Mufflers reduce the noise caused by this combustion.

Transmission Engine power is transmitted (sent) to the wheels through the transmission, drive shaft, and differential. Together, these parts are called the drive train. A part called a clutch links the power in the crankshaft with the drive train. The clutch can be mechanical or hydraulic. Mechanical clutches are operated by a foot pedal. Hydraulic clutches operate automatically by fluid pressure. (*See* CLUTCH.) The transmission contains gears of different sizes. (*See* GEAR.) Manual transmissions require the driver to change gears by moving the gearshift lever. Automatic transmissions do away with clutch pedals and gearshift levers. Gears are shifted automatically by means of hydraulic pressure. (*See* HYDRAULICS.) Cars start forward slowly in low gear. Second gear picks up speed. High gear maintains driving, or cruising, speed. Some cars have four or five sets of forward gears.

The drive shaft carries the power from the transmission to the differential. The differential is a set of gears that drives the wheels. When an automobile goes around a corner, the outside wheel must turn faster because it has a greater distance to travel than the inside wheel. The differential is designed to allow the wheels to turn at different speeds.

Steering, braking, suspension The driver uses the steering wheel to guide the car. The steering wheel turns the steering column. The steering column is linked to the front wheels by a steering box that contains a set of gears. The gears make it easier for the driver to turn the heavy front wheels. Some cars are equipped with power steering. This allows hydraulic pressure to aid the driver.

Automobiles are required by law to have dual braking systems for safety. The main braking system, operated by a foot pedal, acts on all four wheels. It is a hydraulic system. When the driver steps on the brake, fluid is pumped from a master cylinder to each wheel. The pressure of the fluid works either a drum or a disk that is attached to each wheel. (*See* BRAKE.) A second braking system, called the parking brake, is operated by a hand lever.

The lever is connected to wires that pull the brake drums or disks against the rear wheels only. The parking brake will hold a parked car on a hill. It does not have the strength to stop a fast-moving car. Automatic transmissions can be set in positions that lock the gears and prevent the wheels from turning. This will keep a car from moving if it is parked on a hill.

The suspension system on most cars consists of heavy springs and shock absorbers. It helps make the ride more comfortable by cushioning the car when it goes over bumps.

Automobile safety Traffic accidents in the United States during recent years have resulted in an average of 50,000 deaths and millions of injuries each year. Many accidents are caused by drivers who drive too fast. A national speed limit of 55 m.p.h. [89 kph] was adopted in the United States in 1974. During the years when it was in effect, the 55 m.p.h. speed limit was credited with saving thousands of lives. In the mid-1980s, the U.S. Congress allowed states to increase the speed limit to 65 m.p.h. [105 kph] on certain roads. The result has been an increase in traffic-related deaths, according to state traffic records.

Other regulations have recently been enacted to try to save lives. For example, most states require small children to be placed in special protective seats while riding in the car. Also, the United States requires certain safety devices be installed on all new cars and trucks sold in the United States. These safety devices include lap belts, shoulder harnesses, shatterproof windows, collapsible steering columns, and impact-resistant bumpers. In the past, many drivers were reluctant to use their lap belts and shoulder harnesses. The result was thousands of injuries and deaths. Most states

Air bags are safety devices that inflate automatically during a crash. The inflated air bag acts as a cushion, protecting the driver or passenger from injury.

have now passed laws requiring drivers and passengers to use their lap belts and shoulder harnesses.

For added protection, some automobile manufacturers are equipping cars with automatic air bags. An air bag is an inflatable, pillowlike cushion that is stored in the steering wheel on the driver's side of the car. Some cars also have an air bag for the front-seat passenger that is stored in the dashboard. Devices in the car detect the rapid deceleration, or slowing down, that occurs during a crash, and the air bag inflates. The air bag cushions the driver's or passenger's body as it is thrust forward. The air bag later deflates. The high degree of protection that air bags can provide has caused many consumer activist groups to work in favor of laws requiring air bags as standard equipment on all automobiles and trucks sold in the United States.

Tires can be another safety feature. Today's tires adhere to road surfaces better and are manufactured to help give better gas mileage. They also last longer. In fact, automobiles in general have become not only safer but more efficient over the years. Improved suspensions and braking systems enable automobiles to handle better than ever. Automobile manufacturers have added steel supports to vital areas of the automobile body. The supports help the body withstand impacts with greater safety for the passengers. Smaller engines that use less fuel have replaced larger ones without sacrificing too much power.

The National Highway Traffic Safety Administration (NHTSA) sets the safety standards for new automobiles. It sometimes orders manufacturers to recall cars that have been found to have safety defects. A car that has been recalled must be repaired by the manufacturer at no charge to the owner.

Automobiles and the environment The widespread use of automobiles has led to serious environmental concerns. The exhaust from automobile engines produces about 20 percent of the carbon dioxide released into the atmosphere every year in the United States. Carbon dioxide is the main gas responsible for the greenhouse effect. In the greenhouse effect, pollution in the atmosphere helps trap the sun's heat. This causes the earth's temperature to rise. (*See* GREENHOUSE EFFECT.)

Automobiles also give off carbon monoxide, nitrogen dioxide, and sulfur dioxide. These pollutants contribute to acid rain and smog. (*See* ACID RAIN; AIR; SMOG.) The running of automobile air conditioners releases chlorofluorocarbons into the air. (*See* CHLOROFLUOROCARBON.) Chlorofluorocarbons destroy the protective ozone layer of the upper stratosphere. (*See* ATMOSPHERE; OZONE.)

In spite of these effects, the use of automobiles is still increasing. Scientists are researching ways to reduce the amount of pollution from automobiles. One of these solutions was the widespread use of unleaded fuel that began in the mid-1970s. Unleaded fuels do not produce as much pollution as fuels with lead. Also, unleaded fuels do not interefere with the devices that reduce other pollutants in exhaust. These devices are required by law in most states as part of the states' emission-control standards. Emission-control standards set the maximum amount of pollution that can be released in automobile exhaust. Car owners must have their cars tested periodically to determine the amount of emissions being released in their exhaust. Other solutions to reduce pollution involve public transportation, ride sharing, and the development of even more efficient engines that require less fuel.

C.C.; P.Q.F.; W.R.P./R.W.L; F.J.M; J.E.P.

AVALANCHE (av'ə lanch') An avalanche is a mass of snow, ice, rock debris, or soil that suddenly starts to slide or fall down a mountain slope. Spring rains, dry warm winds, and vibrations caused by loud noises and earthquakes can start an avalanche.

To prevent the loss of life to skiers and mountain climbers, Switzerland pioneered devices for testing areas for avalanches. In the United States, avalanches are watched for by the Forest Service of the Department of Agriculture.

The largest avalanche in North America, the Hope Slide, took place in the Cascade Mountains of Canada in 1965. In it, 140,000,000 tons [127,092,000 metric tons] of rock and mud fell 3,900 ft. [1,200 m] to cover part of the British Columbian highway. The avalanche buried three moving cars. The Hope Slide was as wide as 2 mi. [3 km] and as deep as 300 ft. [90 m].   S.A.B./W.R.S.

AVES *See* BIRD.

AVIATION, HISTORY OF Aviation (ā'vē-ā'shən) is the science of designing, developing, building, and flying aircraft. As long ago as the 1500s, the Italian Leonardo da Vinci designed wings that would flap for a person to use in flight. However, as far as we know, Leonardo never built a full-size model for flying. He also designed helicopters and parachutes. The Montgolfier brothers, of France, were the first human beings on record to fly. Their first flight, in 1783, was in a hot-air balloon. (*See* BALLOON.)

The first flight in aviation history was taken in a hot-air balloon in 1783 by the Montgolfier brothers. An artist's sketch of their balloon is shown.

Above is the biplane (double-winged plane) in which Orville Wright made the first successful powered flight in aviation history, at Kitty Hawk, North Carolina, in 1903.

In the early 1800s, Sir George Cayley, an English scientist, developed and flew the first glider. He was the first person to recognize that fixed, curved wings are better than flapping wings for heavier-than-air craft. Cayley became known as "The Father of Aviation." At about the same time, a Frenchman, Henri Giffard, built a cigar-shaped balloon capable of carrying a person. It was filled with hydrogen gas and powered by a steam engine that turned a propeller. In the 1800s, Otto Lilienthal, of Germany, and Octave Chanute and Samuel Langley, of the United States, improved upon gliders.

In 1903, two American brothers, Wilbur and Orville Wright, built an aircraft powered by a home-built gasoline engine that drove a propeller. On December 17, 1903, Orville Wright made the first successful powered flight at Kitty Hawk, North Carolina. The airplane was named *Flyer*. It stayed in the air for twelve seconds. (*See* WRIGHT BROTHERS.)

In 1909, a Frenchman, Louis Bleriot, flew a plane of his own design from France to England, across the English Channel. Lighter-than-air craft were still being developed at that time. Count Ferdinand von Zeppelin, of Germany, built a huge, metal-framed airship called a dirigible. The balloon was filled with hydrogen. The dirigible carried passengers and was powered by several engines. The name *Zeppelin* became synonymous with dirigible. (*See* DIRIGIBLE.)

World War I (1914-1918) brought about many new developments in aviation. Dirigibles were used for observation and for bombing missions. Planes of all shapes and sizes were built for military use even though they were not thought of as major weapons at that time. Most designs featured two wings, one placed over the other. They were called biplanes. Triplanes had three wings. With the introduction of metal construction, single-wing planes, or monoplanes, started to come into use toward the end of World War I. Fighter planes and scout planes had one engine. Machine guns were mounted on most planes. They were timed to fire through the spinning propeller without hitting it. Aerial fights between planes became known as "dogfights." Larger planes, called bombers, had two or three engines.

In 1919, the first commercial airline was started. Air Transport and Travel, Ltd., carried passengers throughout England in modified DeHavilland bombers.

In the 1920s, airmail routes were started in the United States. "Barnstorming" pilots toured the country in their planes, introducing aviation to small towns and cities. They put on flying shows and took people for plane rides. In 1923, Juan del la Cierva, of Spain, designed and flew the first autogyro. It was a forerunner to the helicopter. (*See* HELICOPTER.) In 1926, Commander Richard Byrd, of the United States, flew an airplane over the North Pole. In 1927, Charles Lindbergh became one of America's heroes when he flew his plane, the *Spirit of St. Louis*, nonstop from New York to Paris in 33½ hours. In 1929, the *Graf Zeppelin*, a German dirigible, flew 21,500 mi. [34,298 km] around the world in just three weeks. The *Graf Zeppelin* was 775 ft. [236.3 m] long.

The air transport industry began to grow in the early 1930s. In the United States, the Ford Trimotor, a passenger plane with three engines, was used by most airlines. Many cities built airports. (*See* AIRPORT.) Airline routes were extended to more and more locations. The Boeing Aircraft Company built the first all-metal passenger plane in 1933. It was a monoplane and had landing gear that could be folded up into the body of the plane during flight. It also had deicing equipment that allowed it to fly at high altitudes and in bad weather. The deicers kept ice from forming on the wings. The Boeing DC-3 transport plane was developed from this model. Thousands of DC-3s were built by Boeing between 1935 and 1945. They were durable and dependable and became a familiar sight in the sky. DC-3s were the most used transport

Some milestones in aviation history: (1) The S.E.5a British fighter plane from World War I (1914-1918), (2) the Soviet MiG-21 combat plane, (3) the German dirigible Graf Zeppelin, (4) the German Heinkel 178 turbojet, and (5) the American P-51 Mustang fighter of World War II (1939-1945).

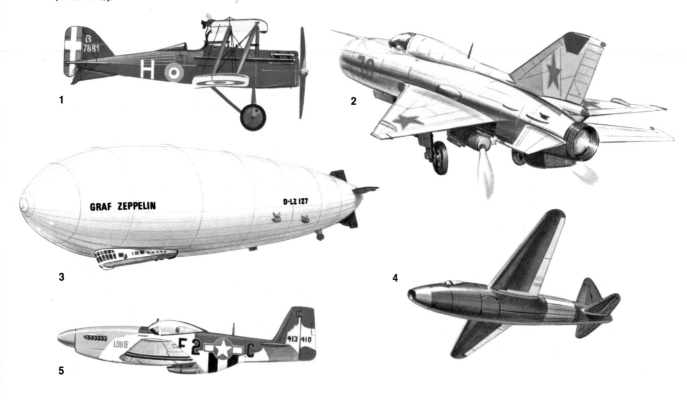

The Concorde, pictured at left, has greatly reduced flying time between Europe and the United States.

planes in the 1940s, especially during World War II (1939-1945), when they were referred to as C-47s. Some DC-3s built in the late 1940s are still flying.

In May 1937, the German dirigible *Hindenburg*, which used hydrogen gas, exploded during a landing at Lakehurst, New Jersey, after a flight across the Atlantic. Many passengers were killed. Commercial dirigible flights were stopped soon after and never resumed. Hot-air balloons owned by individuals and advertising blimps are the only lighter-than-air craft in use today. Blimps are similar to dirigibles in shape. They are like balloons in that they do not have interior framework and they do use helium, a gas that does not burn. Blimps are much smaller than dirigibles.

World War II brought many new developments in aviation. The airplane became a major weapon of war for the first time. Bombers were used against enemy targets. Fighter planes were able to attack fairly close to the ground as well as in the air. "Air power," as it was called, played a large part in the Allies' victory over Germany and Japan.

During the war, aircraft manufacturers expanded their plants in order to meet military needs. Assembly lines were set up so that large numbers of planes could be built quickly. In the United States, fifty thousand planes a year were built. New materials were used that

improved the quality of airplanes. Larger and more powerful engines let planes fly faster and higher. Fighter planes flew at 300 to 400 m.p.h. [480 to 640 kph]. Jet engines were developed toward the end of the war but did not come into wide use until after 1945.

Aviation today The air transport industry has continued to grow. There are now thousands of airports in the United States. Many jet airliners fly at about 600 m.p.h. [960 kph], and jets carry a total of more than 200 million passengers each year. Special electronic equipment allows planes to be flown safely in almost any kind of weather.

Today, so-called jumbo jets can carry up to five hundred passengers. Such planes also carry cargo. The *Concorde*, a passenger airliner developed by the British and the French, can fly about 1,500 m.p.h. [2,400 kph]. It has cut flying time between Europe and the United States to about three hours.

Many business firms whose executives travel a great deal found that they could save money by owning their own planes. Although these planes are usually smaller than commercial jets, many of them fly as fast as commercial airliners and have navigation instruments similar to those of the 'arger planes.

Throughout the history of aviation, interest in recreational flying has always been high. Many people own their own planes just

Modern gliders can soar thousands of feet above the earth for hours.

for the thrill of being able to fly. Usually these privately owned planes are small, propeller-driven craft that can carry two to four people. A new kind of recreational airplane also has become popular. These are the ultralights, gliderlike planes with a small engine, wings, and a seat or harness to hold the pilot.

Perhaps the most important advance in aviation since the jet engine was the successful testing of the space shuttle *Columbia*. The space shuttle is the first reusable spacecraft. It is launched like a rocket but lands like an airplane. Between April 1981 and November 1984, fourteen flights were made. The first four were made to find out how well the space shuttle would work. On later flights, communications satellites were repaired in space, and new ones were launched. Eventually, the space shuttle may have many uses, including carrying people from one space station to another.

In the mid-1970s, when the cost of oil rose sharply, commercial and cargo transport airlines were seriously affected. Higher fuel costs meant that unless the large airplanes flew at full capacity all the time, they would not be profitable. Most of the major airlines and manufacturers seemed to agree on the need for a fuel-efficient transport that would carry 150 to 200 passengers. The first of these, the Boeing 757 and 767, began operating in 1982.

The United States government regulates aviation through the Federal Aviation Administration (FAA). The FAA is responsible for overseeing safety and progress in aviation. *See also* AERODYNAMICS; AERONAUTICS; AIRPLANE; SPACE TRAVEL.

W.R.P./J.VP.

AVOCADO (äv′ə käd′ō) An avocado is a fruit grown from a tree of the same name. The tree belongs to the family Lauraceae. It was originally found in tropical South America. The avocado is now planted in warm regions around the world. The fruit is pear-shaped with a green, thick skin. The flesh is yellow green and coarse. It is often eaten in sandwiches or salads or used to make a food called guacamole. The fruit is also called an alligator pear.   S.R.G./T.L.G.; F.W.S.

AVOCET (av′ə set′) An avocet is a wading bird that belongs to the family Recurvirostridae. There are four species of avocets. One is found in North America. The others are found in South America, Australia, and Eurasia. The avocet lives along the shoreline. It feeds by swinging its curved beak through shallow water. It eats small insects and crustaceans.   S.R.G./L.S.

Avocets are long-legged wading birds. The upward-curving bill of this bird is a special adaptation for feeding under the water.

AVOGADRO, AMEDEO (1776-1856) Amedeo Avogadro was an Italian physicist who made several important discoveries about molecules. In 1811, he stated that equal volumes of any gases at the same temperature and pressure contain the same number of molecules. This statement, known as Avogadro's law, is a principle used in a method of finding atomic weights.

A mole is the molecular weight of a substance stated in grams. One mole of any substance contains 6.023×10^{23} molecules. This number is called Avogadro's constant or Avogadro's number. Avogadro was the first person to tell the difference between an atom and a molecule. This difference was necessary to obtain correct values for atomic weights and molecular weights. However,

not until after Avogadro's death was his work accepted. *See also* ATOMIC WEIGHT; MOLE (UNIT); MOLECULAR WEIGHT.   J.J.A./D.G.F.

AXIL (ak′səl) The axil is the angle between the upper part of a leaf or leaf stem and the branch from which it is growing. The axil is located just above the node. Branches, flowers, leaves, or thorns grow from buds, which form at the nodes. In some plants, such as the lily, the axil may produce buds that can be used to grow a new plant. *See also* PLANT KINGDOM.   A.J.C./M.H.S.

AZIMUTH (az′məth) Azimuth is the position or bearing of an object on earth or in the sky in relation to a fixed point, usually north. It is measured as an angle from 0° to 360°.

In sea navigation, the stars are used to figure out an azimuth. This lets sailors know where they are in the ocean. Surveyors and mapmakers also use azimuths. *See also* NAVIGATION.   A.J.C./C.R.

B

BABBAGE, CHARLES (1792-1871) Charles Babbage was an English mathematician whose work helped lead to the development of the modern computer. Babbage began developing his first computing machine, the difference engine, in the early 1820s. However, the necessary precision machine tools and knowledge about electric circuits were unavailable, so Babbage's efforts were unsuccessful. His vision of a computing machine of vast power was a bold step, however. Babbage also invented the speedometer.   A.J.C./D.G.F.; R.J.S.

Baboons are large monkeys found in Africa and the Arabian Peninsula. They live in closely knit family groups, as pictured.

BABOON (ba bün′) A baboon is a large monkey found in the rocky regions, open woodlands, and plains of Africa and the Arabian Peninsula. The baboon has a large head and long, sharp teeth. A baboon's arms are about the same length as its legs. A male baboon is much larger than a female baboon.

Baboons can carry food in pouches that are inside their cheeks. They feed on vegetables, fruit, grass, insects, leaves, and roots. Baboons are social animals, living in groups of from ten to one hundred. A large male usually rules. Male baboons, regarded as tough fighters, have been known to attack leopards.

The male hamadryas baboon of the Arabian Peninsula, Ethiopia, Egypt, Sudan, and Somalia has long, gray hair on its head and shoulders. The chacma baboon of South Africa has grayish brown hair on its body and a long collar of hair, or ruff, around its neck.

J.J.A./J.J.M.

BABYLONIAN CIVILIZATION One of the greatest of the ancient civilizations developed about 4,000 years ago around a city called Babylon, located in what is now Iraq. The city was the capital of the empire of Babylonia, and its civilization is called Babylonian (bab′ə-lō′nyən). The 1,500 years of Babylonian civilization, lasting from 2000 to 500 B.C., produced important advances in astronomy, mathematics, architecture, engineering, writing, and law. Between 600 and 500 B.C.,

Babylon became the largest city in the world. It was a major center of science, art, commerce, and religion.

The root of the progress made by the people of Babylonian civilization was cuneiform writing, a system of characters that organized communication. The wedge-shaped characters of cuneiform writing were placed at various angles and in groups of two to thirty. This system of written symbols permitted the Babylonians to write books, record history, and promote education and libraries. The Babylonians created a vast literature. Some of the myths of Babylonia are very similar to some parts of the Bible, such as the stories of the creation of the earth and the great flood. About 1750 B.C., Babylonian civilization produced what was probably the world's first written code of law. Called the *Code of Hammurabi*, it was named after a king of Babylonia. Archeologists examining the ruins of Babylon found the code inscribed on a column of the king's palace. They also found more than 150,000 clay tablets inscribed with cuneiform writing.

In astronomy and mathematics, the Babylonians had great success. Their records show that they divided a circle into 360 degrees and an hour into 60 minutes. Also, they had knowledge of fractions, square roots, and square numbers. The Babylonians recorded their observations of the sky and were able to predict eclipses of the moon.

With their capital spread out on both sides of a river and their economic life based on agriculture, the Babylonians learned how to build bridges, aqueducts, and irrigation canals. Their engineering skills involved maps and surveys that required leveling instruments and measuring rods. The Babylonians constructed sanitary and drainage systems. They even had a kind of farmer's almanac to improve their agriculture.

Babylonian builders were responsible for the construction of two of the most marvelous buildings of ancient times. The ziggurat, a seven-story temple-tower of baked brick, is linked by legend with the biblical Tower of Babel. Under their greatest king, Nebuchadnezzar II, the Babylonians built the Hanging Gardens, which the ancient Greeks called one of the Seven Wonders of the World. Within Babylon were many splendid structures, especially the palaces of the kings and the temples of the gods.

The Babylonian empire came to an end when Babylon was conquered by the Persians under Cyrus the Great in 539 B.C. Until the nineteenth century, scholars and scientists depended on writings from ancient Greece for their information on Babylonian civilization. During the past one hundred years, archeologists and other scientists have greatly increased existing knowledge of Babylonian civilization. Examples of Babylonian science and art are found in several of the leading museums of the United States and Europe. *See also* ARCHEOLOGY.   G.M.B./S.O.

Backswimmers use their long rear legs as oars.

BACKSWIMMER The backswimmers are also called boat bugs. They are one of many types of water bugs. Although backswimmers spend most of their lives in the water, they are able to fly long distances. These insects are small, usually 0.118 to 0.669 in. [3 to 17 mm] in length. They use their long, flat hind legs to paddle through the water. They usually swim on their backs. Their short front legs are used for holding prey. Backswimmers hold a bubble of air between their wings and body. They use the air in the bubble for breathing when they are underwater. This lets them stay underwater for as long as six hours. Backswimmers spend the winter buried in the mud at the bottom of a pond or stream.

Backswimmers have sharp beaks, which they use for stabbing fish and other small water animals. They suck the juices out of their victims. Backswimmers can also give painful bites to people.   A.J.C./J.R.

BACON, FRANCIS (1561-1626) Francis Bacon was an English philosopher and statesman who developed a scientific method for solving problems. Bacon felt that people should have control over the world around them. The way to get this control, he believed, is through knowledge, and the way to get knowledge is through science.

Bacon stated that there are several things that keep people from getting knowledge. First, people tend to decide something is generally true if they have found it to be true in only one or two cases. They do not test it to find out if it is true in all cases. Second, people base decisions on their own backgrounds and educations. They do not consider that someone with a different background and education might make a different decision. Third, people have to use words to describe something. Because words can be confusing, it is important to be exact in a description. Bacon called these blocks of knowledge *prejudices*.

Once these prejudices are put aside, Bacon said, people can obtain knowledge through inductive reasoning. Inductive reasoning involves making many observations and tests before arriving at any conclusions. Bacon suggested that lists be prepared. One list is for things that are true. A second list is for things that are not true. A third list is for things that are more true than not. For example, suppose a person has seen only red apples. He or she says, "All apples are red." The person believes this until he or she sees a yellow apple. The person may then say, "Most apples are red." If the person had made lists as suggested by Bacon, he or she would find that there are many red apples and many yellow apples. It would be better to say, "There are red apples and yellow apples." Bacon's theory states that the more often an idea is tested and found to be true, the more likely it is to be true.

Sir Francis Bacon

Because Bacon was highly respected as a philosopher, his views were widely accepted. His work helped greatly in the progress of Renaissance science. *See also* INDUCTION (LOGICAL).   A.J.C./D.G.F.

BACTERIA CELL

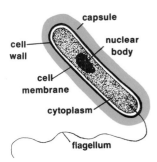

Shown is a diagram of a bacterium. This one-celled organism gets everything it needs for life directly from its environment. The single flagellum provides movement.

BACTERIA (bak tir′ē ə) Bacteria (singular: *bacterium*) are one-celled organisms. They are among the smallest and most widespread of all living things. They may live alone or in groups called colonies. Bacteria belong to the kingdom Monera. Bacteria, or something like them, were probably the first living organisms on earth. (*See* EVOLUTION.) They reproduce so quickly that one bacterium can produce millions of others in only a few hours.

Structure and life of bacteria Most bacterial cells have a strong cell wall. Many bacteria have a capsule, a coating surrounding the cell wall. Some bacteria are able to move only by floating passively in the air or water. Most others, though, can move under their own power. Some wriggle from one place to another, while others use a whiplike flagellum to swim. (*See* FLAGELLUM.)

Bacteria have one of four shapes. Since they are so small, their shapes can only be seen with a microscope. The coccus (plural, *cocci*) is round. The bacillus (plural, *bacilli*) is rod shaped. The vibrio (plural, *vibrios*) is shaped like a boomerang. The spirillum (plural, *spirilla*) is spiral shaped.

Bacteria usually reproduce by fission. (*See* ASEXUAL REPRODUCTION.) In fission, the organism splits into two new organisms. It is by rapid fission that bacteria are able to reproduce in such great numbers. At times, bacteria may exchange DNA and other genetic material in a type of sexual reproduction. (*See* DNA.) Some bacteria produce endospores for reproduction. (*See* ENDOSPORE.) These endospores are very strong. They are often able to survive for extended periods of time in unfavorable conditions.

Bacteria may live in soil, in water, in air, or in other organisms. Although most bacteria live in temperatures between 50 to 104°F. [10 to 40°C], some require either very hot or very cold temperatures in order to grow and reproduce. Some bacteria are aerobic and require air to live. (*See* AEROBE.) Other bac-

Bacteria are classified according to their shape. One bacterium can produce millions of others like it in just a few hours.

FOUR TYPES OF BACTERIA

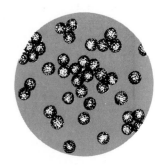

Spirilla are spiral shaped.

Vibrios are shaped like boomerangs.

Bacilli are rod shaped.

Cocci are round.

teria are anaerobic and do not require air to live. (*See* ANAEROBE.) Often, anaerobic bacteria die if they are exposed to air.

Some bacteria produce their own food by photosynthesis. (*See* PHOTOSYNTHESIS.) Others use chemicals as food. Some bacteria are parasites and rely on other living organisms called hosts for food. Some of these parasites harm their hosts, while others live in a state of mutualism. (*See* SYMBIOSIS.) Some bacteria are saprophytes and get their food from dead organisms. (*See* SAPROPHYTE.) These saprophytic bacteria are important parts of the food chain and of other cycles involving carbon, nitrogen, oxygen, and sulfur. (*See* FOOD CHAIN.) Underground oil and natural gas deposits may be the result of the work done by saprophytic bacteria millions of years ago.

Helpful bacteria Most bacteria are useful to humans. Certain bacteria are needed to make cheese, yogurt, and butter. Some bacteria are used in the treatment of sewage and garbage. These bacteria release methane gas as they digest the wastes. In fact, there are cities in the United States and in Europe that use these bacteria as the source of their entire energy supply. One newly discovered type of bacteria can be used to clean up oil spills in the oceans. Still other helpful bacteria live in the human body. Some help prevent infections, while others aid in digestion.

Harmful bacteria Some bacteria are harmful to humans. Some can cause food spoilage. This may result in botulism or other forms of food poisoning. (*See* BOTULISM; FOOD POISONING.) Some bacteria are pathogenic, or disease causing. Some cause diseases in plants that can destroy entire fields of crops. Some bacteria cause sicknesses in animals, including human beings. Some of the human diseases

Some bacteriologists (scientists who study bacteria) work to prevent and cure the diseases that certain bacteria cause.

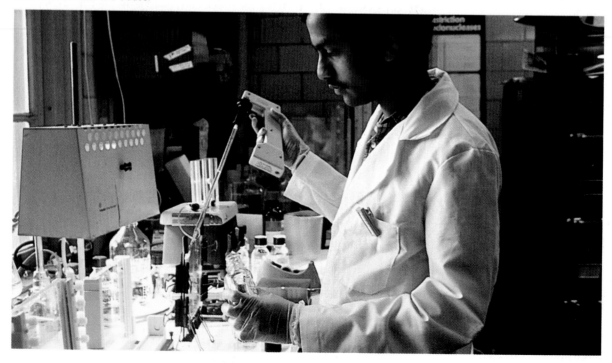

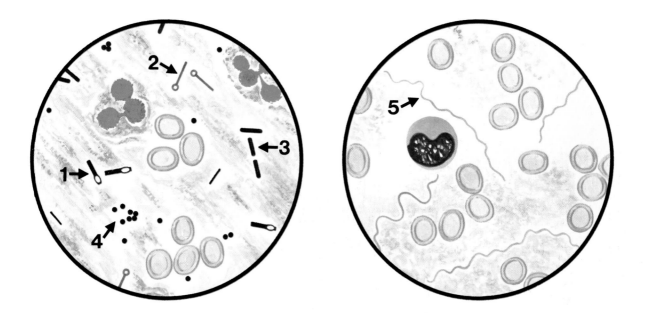

Two microscopic views of human blood show harmful bacteria. (1) Clostridium tetani are the cause of tetanus, or lockjaw. (2) and (3) are other types of Clostridia. Notice that (1) and (2) have endospores, seen as rounded swellings, whereas (3) does not. (4) indicates a group of staphylococci. Staphylococci can cause boils and blood poisoning. The blood on the right (5) shows Borellia recurrentis, the bacterium that causes relapsing fever.

caused by bacteria are tuberculosis, tetanus, leprosy, syphilis, and gonorrhea. Some bacterial diseases can be fought successfully by the body's own defenses. Vaccinations can help the body build up certain antibodies to prevent a sickness or to make it less severe. (*See* IMMUNITY.) Certain drugs attack only bacteria. (*See* ANTIBIOTIC.) The use of antibiotics and sulfa drugs has done much to help control the spread and danger of bacterial diseases and epidemics. *See also* DISEASE; INFECTION; KOCH, ROBERT; PASTEUR, LOUIS.

A.J.C./E.R.L.

BACTERIOLOGY *See* MICROBIOLOGY.

BACTERIOPHAGE (bak tir′ē ə faj′) A bacteriophage is any virus that attacks bacteria. The word *bacteriophage* means "bacteria eater." A bacteriophage, like all viruses, is acellular—that is, not a cell. It is made up of a nucleic acid and a protein covering. (*See* BACTERIA; VIRUS.)

Bacteriophages are of many different shapes and sizes. Some bacteriophages have hollow, rod-shaped "tails" and sphere- or T-shaped "heads." Others are threadlike. The heads contain nucleic acids. (*See* NUCLEIC ACID.) The infection of a bacterial cell by a tailed virus involves attachment of the bacteriophage tail to the cell wall of the bacterium. Then the nucleic acid is injected through the tail into the bacterium. The genetic information in this nucleic acid causes other bacteriophages to be formed inside the bacterium. If the bacterium dies, the new bacteriophages are released and attack other bacteria. Bacteriophages that do not kill the host bacterium may help it to become resistant to certain drugs. Scientists often use bacteriophages to help them understand heredity.

A.J.C./M.J.C.; E.R.L.

BADGER (baj′ər) The badger is a mammal that is a member of the family Mustelidae. (*See* MAMMAL.) The family also includes the weasel, skunk, and otter. One species of badger is found in North America, while another species lives in Europe and northern Asia.

Badgers live in holes that they dig in the ground. A badger is a heavyset animal with short legs, short ears, and a doglike head. It grows to lengths of 2 ft. [60 cm]. The fur of the badger is silvery gray with black-and-white

Badgers, such as the one above, are burrowing animals. They usually come out of the holes in which they live only at night.

markings on the head. Badgers are omnivorous, eating many different plants and animals. (*See* OMNIVORE.) Much of the badger's food is small mammals, such as mice, which it hunts at night. The badger is not very fast but fights fiercely when attacked. The fur of the badger was once used to make paintbrushes, shaving brushes, and coat trimmings. However, synthetic (human-made) materials have largely replaced badger fur for these purposes.

S.R.G./J.J.M.

BAEKELAND, LEO (1863-1944) Leo Baekeland was an American chemist known for the invention of Bakelite, an early plastic. Baekeland was born in Ghent, Belgium. He moved to the United States in 1889.

In 1891, Baekeland invented a sensitive photographic paper. Eastman Kodak bought it from him for one million dollars. Baekeland then tried to invent a synthetic substitute for shellac. He experimented with resins made from phenol and formaldehyde. (*See* RESIN; SHELLAC.) In 1909, he produced a resin that was resistant to water and solvents, was an electric insulator, and was easy to shape and cut. Bakelite, named after him, was the first synthetic resin as well as the first thermosetting plastic. *See also* BAKELITE.   J.J.A./D.G.F.

BAKELITE (bā′kə līt′) Bakelite, called phenolic resin by chemists, is a plastic made from phenol and formaldehyde. It was the first truly synthetic plastic. Bakelite was put into commercial use by 1916. It is a thermosetting plastic, one that sets when heated and cannot be molded. Bakelite is dark in color. It is widely used because it resists heat and is comparatively cheap to produce.

Bakelite was once used for the handles of kettles, pans, and irons. It is also a good electric insulator. It is used in the electrical industry and in the home for light switches, plugs, and other electrical fittings. Another use of Bakelite is in laminations with wood, fabric, and other materials to make tough, heat-proof substances. The invention of Bakelite opened the door to modern plastics. *See also* BAEKELAND, LEO; PLASTIC.   J.J.A./J.M.

BALANCE (bal′əns) A balance is an accurate device used to measure the weight of chemicals and other substances in a laboratory. It consists of a horizontal bar balanced on a thin edge of metal. A pointer attached to the bar moves when the bar is tilted in either direction. Small pans are suspended from each end of the bar. The substance to be weighed is placed in one pan. Numbered weights of different sizes are placed in the other pan. When the weight in both pans is equal, the bar is horizontal, and the pointer is motionless. The weight of the substance can be found by adding up the weights needed to balance the pans.

Laboratory balances are delicate instruments. They are kept in glass cases to protect them against moisture and gases in the air. Balances must be adjusted for temperature and moisture before each use. Electric balances and electric microbalances are used for even more accurate measurements. *See also* WEIGHT.   W.R.P./R.W.L.

BALD EAGLE The bald eagle (ē′gəl), also called the white-headed eagle (*Haliaetus leucocephalus*), is a large, North American bird of prey. It is the national bird of the United States. The adult bald eagle reaches a length of 30 to 35 in. [75 to 90 cm], a wingspread of 6.6 ft. [2 m], and a weight of 7.7 to 14.3 lb. [3.5 to 6.5 kg]. Bald eagles may live as long as thirty years. They have very sharp eyes and can spot prey from great heights.

The bald eagle is brown and has white feathers on its head and tail. These white head feathers are what make the eagle look bald.

The bald eagle is the national emblem of the United States (below left). It is in danger of extinction and so is protected. The young eagle chick is being reared in captivity and will be released into the wild to help increase the bald eagle population (below right).

Although the bald eagle was once found throughout North America, most of the 2,400 remaining birds are in Alaska. Because bald eagles usually eat fish and other small animals, Alaskan hunters killed more than 100,000 bald eagles between 1917 and 1952 to protect the salmon and fur industries. The bald eagle is now protected by federal law.

Currently, a major threat to bald eagles is pesticides. These chemicals concentrate in the bird's body, causing it to lay infertile or weak-shelled eggs or produce deformed young. A.J.C./L.S.

BALLISTICS (bə lis′tiks) Ballistics is the science concerned with the motion and behavior of projectiles, such as bullets, bombs, rockets, and guided missiles. The three main branches of ballistics are interior, exterior, and terminal ballistics.

Interior ballistics deals with the motion of a projectile as it travels down the barrel of a weapon, such as a rifle or pistol. The weight of the bullet, the pressure placed on the bullet, the speed at which the bullet moves through the barrel, the barrel's length and diameter, and the speed at which the bullet leaves the barrel all affect the flight of the bullet. A person who studies the interior ballistics of a rifle or pistol has to know all these things. The interior ballistics of missiles is concerned with the design of rocket engines and the choice of propellants. A rocket is propelled by the reaction to expanding gases escaping from it.

The speed at which a projectile leaves a gun barrel or a missile leaves a launch is called the initial velocity. The initial velocity of the projectiles of some rifles is 5,000 ft. [1,500 m] per second. The initial velocity of missiles is lower because most missiles are much heavier than a bullet.

Exterior ballistics is concerned with the flight path, or trajectory, of a projectile from the time it leaves the rifle or gun until landing. After a bullet has left the gun, it travels in an arc, falling downward because of gravity. The amount of air resistance to a projectile depends on the projectile's size, shape, and speed, and on the density of air. Air resistance slows the projectile, reducing the range, or distance it travels. Winds and crosswinds can affect the range and direction of a projectile. If a projectile is fired from a moving weapon, or if the target is moving, the range can be affected. Electronic computers are used to measure the effects of all these factors.

Terminal ballistics is concerned with the effect of the projectile when it reaches its target. Bullets cause damage by penetration. Shell or bomb damage is caused by explosion. Nuclear missiles produce blast, heat, and radiation.

Forensic ballistics is a separate field that helps police identify bullets. Every gun or rifle makes marks on the bullets it fires. No other gun or rifle can make the same marks on a bullet. Experts can find out whether or not a particular bullet was fired from a particular gun. Forensic ballistics has greatly aided police officers in identifying and arresting armed robbers and murderers. *See also* GUN; MISSILE. J.J.A./J.T.

BALLOON (bə lün′) A balloon is a bag filled with hot air or a gas. A balloon rises and floats because the hot air or gas in the balloon is lighter than the air outside. Light materials, such as silk or plastic, are used in making balloons that carry passengers or materials of some kind. Such balloons may be either captive or free floating. A captive balloon is anchored to the ground by a line called a

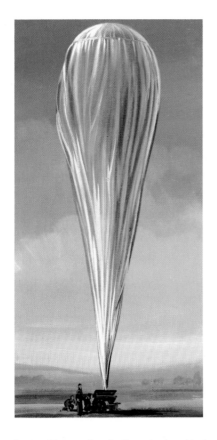

A scientific weather balloon is about to be launched (above left). It contains special instruments to study conditions in the atmosphere. Balloons were used by Union forces during the Civil War (1861-1865) to observe Confederate troops (right). Filled with hydrogen on the ground, many of the balloons trailed telegraph wires through which their crews could communicate with troops on the ground.

tether. A free-floating balloon travels in whatever direction the wind blows it. Many balloons have a gondola, or basket, attached below to carry passengers and equipment.

The first practical hot-air balloon was developed in France by two brothers, Joseph and Etienne Montgolfier. Their balloon was made of cloth and paper and had a diameter of about 35 ft. [11 m]. They first flew the balloon on June 5, 1783. The first people to fly in a free-floating balloon were Jean-Francois Pilatre de Rozier and Francois Laurent. They made their flight outside Paris in November, 1783. The following month, J.A.C. Charles and Nicolas Louis Robert made the world's first flight in a hydrogen-filled balloon. They rose to about 2,000 ft. [610 m] and traveled about 25 mi. [40 km].

There are two kinds of balloons—gas and hot-air. The main kinds of gas balloons are superpressure balloons, zero-pressure balloons, and expandable balloons. All three are used for scientific purposes.

In a superpressure balloon, the gas inside has a greater pressure than that of the air outside. When a superpressure balloon is launched, the bag is partly filled and then is sealed. The gas expands as the balloon rises. The bag of a superpressure balloon is not flexible, so once the bag is filled, the balloon does not go any higher. Superpressure balloons can stay in the air for many months.

The gas inside a zero-pressure balloon is at the same pressure as that of the air on the outside. Once the balloon is aloft, the gas expands. If the gas expands too much, the excess gas escapes through a valve. In order to keep zero-pressure balloons in the air, ballast (a load of material carried just for this purpose) must be released from time to time. This is done by radio signals from the ground. Zero-pressure balloons usually fly for several days.

Expandable balloons are about 6 ft. [2 m] across when they lift off. As the balloon rises and the gas expands, the bag may expand to about 20 ft. [6 m]. When the balloon reaches the proper height, the bag bursts, and its instruments are returned to earth by parachute.

Gas balloons may be filled with hydrogen, helium, or natural gas. Natural gas is by far the cheapest, but it has the least lifting ability. Helium costs more than natural gas, but it is nonflammable (that is, it will not catch fire) and therefore very safe. Hydrogen has the greatest lifting ability, because it is the lightest

Large commercial balloons, such as the Goodyear balloon, are usually filled with helium (above). Amateur hot-air ballooning is a popular sport in many areas (below).

gas. However, hydrogen can be dangerous because it is highly combustible (capable of catching fire).

Hot-air balloons work much the same way that gas balloons do. The air in the bag is heated, making it lighter than the air outside. The air is heated by a propane-gas burner mounted below the bag. To make the balloon rise, more propane is burned. To lose altitude, less gas is burned.

Balloons have been used in wars. For example, balloons were used by France in a war in 1870. They were also used in the Civil War, World War I, and World War II. For the most part, captive balloons were used to observe the enemy's troops.

Much of the information we get about the weather is obtained from instruments carried by balloons. Weather researchers, or meteorologists, release balloons into the atmosphere to study the temperature, humidity, and pressure of the air at various altitudes. They use this information to forecast the weather. (*See* METEOROLOGY.) Balloons are also sent high into the stratosphere (the second layer of the atmosphere above the earth) carrying instruments to record conditions such as cosmic radiation. (*See* COSMIC RAYS.) These balloons may also carry telescopes and cameras. They have gone up as high as 27 mi. [43.5 km].

Sport balloonists use both gas and hot-air balloons. Balloon races and rallies are held in many parts of the country. To get a ballooning license from the Federal Aviation Administration (FAA), a person must be at least sixteen years old, pass a written examination, and have ten hours of flying time with an instructor.

The record for the highest flight in a helium-filled balloon was set in 1961 by two U.S. Navy officers—Commander Malcolm Ross and Lieutenant Commander Victor A. Prather, Jr. In the balloon *Lee Lewis Memorial*, they rose 113,739.9 ft. [34,668 m].

The first people to cross the Atlantic Ocean in a balloon were Maxie Anderson,

Ben Abruzzo, and Larry Newman. In August 1978, in the *Double Eagle II*, they lifted off from Presque Isle, Maine. They landed in Misery, France, slightly over 137 hours later. They had traveled 3,107 mi. [5,000 km].

In June 1988, Per Linstrand of the United Kingdom set the record for the highest flight in a hot-air balloon when he rose to an altitude of 65,000 ft. [19,812 m] above Plano, Texas. *See also* AVIATION, HISTORY OF.

J.J.A.; P.Q.F./J.VP.; L.W.

BALSAM (bȯl′səm) Balsam is an aromatic resin that comes from some herbs and trees. (*See* RESIN.) Balsam is used mainly in the making of medicine, paint, perfume, and incense. Some balsams flow naturally from herbs and trees. Other balsams must be gotten by cutting or breaking open herbs and trees. In North America, Canada balsam is taken from fir trees.

G.M.B./M.H.S.

BAMBOO (bam′bü′) Bamboo is a member of the grass family, Gramineae. Bamboos are native to tropical climates. Growing from an underground stem called a rhizome, they grow very rapidly. Most bamboos are very tall—some as high as 120 ft. [37 m]—and as thick as 1 ft. [30 cm]. Bamboos have hollow wood stems. The leaves fall off as the plant grows. Some bamboos blossom once in thirty years. Others may take one hundred years to blossom. A bamboo plant dies after it blooms. The seeds from the blossoms grow into new plants.

Bamboo is used to make many products. Some fishing poles are made from the stems of the plant. Bamboo stems are also used to make rafts, furniture, and fences. In some countries, the young stems and rhizomes are pickled and eaten.

S.A.E./M.J.C.; M.H.S.

Bananas grow in bunches on plants in hot, damp climates, such as in parts of Central and South America.

BANANA (bə nan′ə) Bananas are plants that grow in tropical regions. They grow 4 to 30 ft. [1.3 to 9 m] in height. The banana plant looks like a palm tree, but it is not a tree. It does not have a woody stem or trunk. Instead, its leaves grow from a tough rootstock by which the plant spreads.

One large flower grows from the central stalk of the plant. This flower develops into the fruit, also called a banana. Each plant has one bunch of bananas, which can weigh as much as 100 lb. [45 kg]. Cultivation of the banana plant has resulted in a fruit that has no seeds. New plants are started from cuttings from old plants.

Bananas are cut while they are green. They are then loaded on trains to be transported to ships that carry them to many parts of the world. During shipment, they begin to mature and turn yellow. Brazil is the leading banana-growing country, producing as much as 5.5 million tons [5 million metric tons] a year. The United States imports more bananas than any other country.

Bananas are a nutritious food. They contain potassium and vitamins A and C and are rich in carbohydrates. Manila hemp is made from the fibers of some banana plants. It is used to make rope and certain fabrics.

P.G.C./F.W.S.

BANDICOOT (ban′di küt′) Bandicoots make up a family of marsupials found in Australia and New Guinea. (*See* MARSUPIAL.) There are nineteen species. These ratlike mammals rarely grow to be larger than 2 ft. [0.6 m]. The second and third toes are grown together. Like all marsupials, the bandicoot carries and nurses its young in a pouch. Only the bandicoot, however, has a pouch that opens at the bottom instead of at the top. The bandicoot is nocturnal. It sleeps in a burrow during the day and comes out to eat plants and insects at night.   A.J.C./R.J.B.

Bandicoots are marsupials that live in Australia and New Guinea. They carry and nurse their young in a pouch.

BANNEKER, BENJAMIN (1731-1806)

Benjamin Banneker was an African-American astronomer, inventor, and mathematician. Banneker also wrote essays. He was born in Ellicott, Maryland, and was educated at a school with both black and white students. Banneker spent most of his life as a tobacco farmer. He learned astronomy and mathematics by teaching himself. When he was in his twenties, he became famous for creating the first working clock made entirely in America. Banneker carved the wheels and gears out of wood. He also published research on bees, did a mathematical study of the life of the seventeen-year locust, and wrote about the need for peace and racial equality.

Banneker is well known for his almanacs, published between 1791 and 1797, which included his astronomical calculations and observations. An almanac is a book containing information about such topics as astronomy and the weather, arranged by the days, weeks, and months of a year. Banneker contributed astronomical calculations for other almanacs until 1802. In 1791, Banneker was invited by George Washington, the first president of the United States, to help survey (measure) the land that would become the capital of the United States, now called Washington, D.C. Banneker was also helpful in planning the placement of streets and buildings in the city. Banneker was the first black to be appointed to an official position by a president.   P.Q.F./L.W.

BANTING, SIR FREDERICK GRANT

(1891-1941) Sir Frederick Banting was a Canadian physician who discovered insulin, a hormone that controls the body's use of sugar. Working with Charles Best and others, Banting discovered this hormone by taking it out of the pancreas. (*See* INSULIN.)

Banting's discovery led to a complete change in the treatment of diabetes mellitus, a disease that occurs because of either the lack of, or the body's inability to use, insulin. (*See* DIABETES.) Banting and a partner, J.J. Macleod, won the 1923 Nobel Prize for medicine for the discovery of insulin. Banting shared his prize with Charles Best, a fellow researcher, a striking example of scientific partnership.   J.J.A./D.G.F.

BANYAN (ban′yən) The banyan is a member of the mulberry family that produces figlike fruits. Its scientific name is *Ficus bengalensis*. It is found in tropical Asia and Africa. The banyan may grow as tall as 115.5 ft. [35 m]. It has roots growing down from its branches into the ground. Some banyans cover 1 acre [0.4 hectare] or more. Some varieties of banyans are epiphytes that grow onto other trees in order to support their roots. *See also* EPIPHYTE. A.J.C./M.H.S.

BARBERRY FAMILY The barberry (bär′-ber′ē) family is a group of about five hundred species of spiny shrubs that are dicotyledons. (*See* DICOTYLEDON.) Barberries grow from 3 to 12 ft. [1 to 3.7 m] high. Barberry shrubs are native to the moderate-climate zones of the northern hemisphere. They are most frequently planted by landscapers for hedges and other landscape features. They have yellow wood and yellow flowers. The berries are red, yellow, blue, purple, or black. The berries of most species can be made into jellies. A yellow dye is found in some of the barberry plants of Asia and South America.

In the United States, the best known kinds of barberries are the common barberry, the Japanese barberry, and the wintergreen barberry. The common barberry is attacked by spring stem rust, which is very harmful to wheat. For this reason, there are laws in the wheat-growing areas of the United States that prohibit the growing of barberry. G.M.B./M.H.S.

BARBITURATE (bär bich′ə rət) A barbiturate is a drug that slows down the activity of the brain and the rest of the nervous system. Barbiturates are sometimes prescribed by doctors to induce sleep or calm people when they suffer from severe anxiety. In the United States, barbiturates can be obtained legally only with a doctor's prescription.

Barbiturates are made from barbituric acid. They come in tablet or capsule form or sometimes as a powder or liquid. Different barbiturates vary in strength and in the length of time that their effects last. Also, different people may have different reactions to taking the same amount of the same barbiturate.

Regular use of barbiturates can lead to addiction. (*See* ADDICTION.) Some people improperly take large amounts of barbiturates to escape tension. Large doses make the user's speech become slurred, and coordination and judgment become poor. A person can die from an overdose of barbiturates. When an addicted person tries to stop taking barbiturates, he or she becomes extremely nervous. His or her body may shake and twitch violently. Abruptly stopping the use of barbiturates can cause death. An addict can usually end his or her dependency on the drugs by gradually reducing the amount taken.

Today, barbiturates are used less frequently for their sleep-inducing and calming effects than are another kind of drug, called benzodiazepines. Benzodiazepines are considered safer and more effective than barbiturates. Barbiturates are now used mostly used to prevent seizures from epilepsy or as anesthetics. (*See* ANESTHETIC; EPILEPSY.) Barbiturates are also occasionally used to relax mentally ill patients, calming them so they can talk over their problems with their doctors.

J.J.A./L.V.C.; J.J.F.

BARIUM (bar′ē əm) Barium is a soft, silvery metallic element. It was discovered in 1808 by Sir Humphry Davy, an English scientist. (*See* DAVY, SIR HUMPHRY; ELEMENT.) Barium is found most often in a mineral called barite. It is extracted from barite by electrolysis. (*See* ELECTROLYSIS.)

Barium is a very reactive metal and is almost never found in a pure state. This is because it reacts with the oxygen in the air. Pure barium has very few uses, but its compounds are widely used. Doctors use barium sulfate in X-ray examinations. The patient whose intestines will be X-rayed takes the barium sulfate by mouth or by means of an enema. The barium sulfate absorbs X rays, and the intestines show up white on the photograph. Barium nitrate is used in fireworks to give a green flame. Barium carbonate is used in ceramics and glass.

Barium's symbol is Ba. Its atomic number is 56. Its atomic weight is 137.3. Barium melts at 1,337°F. [725°C] and boils at 2,984°F. [1,640°C]. Its relative density is 3.5. *See also* RELATIVE DENSITY. M.E./J.R.W.

BARK Bark is the protective outer covering of tree branches, trunks, and roots. Bark has three layers. The outer periderm is made mostly of dead tissue called cork. The periderm is usually thick. It protects the tree against weather, insects, and disease. The middle cortex layer is made of living but non-growing cells. The innermost phloem carries food made in the tree's leaves down to the roots. The periderm of some trees has small openings called lenticels. Lenticels allow gases such as carbon dioxide and oxygen to enter and leave the plant.

People use bark mainly for its cork. Quinine, cough medicine, cinnamon, and other useful substances are also obtained from bark. *See also* CORK; CORTEX; PHLOEM; QUININE. A.J.C./M.H.S.

The bark of some trees is valuable. Cinnamon, a spice that has been used since ancient times, is made from the bark of the cinnamon tree (above). Bark helps protect trees. For example, the thick bark of slash pines (below) helps insulate the trees from the heat of forest fires.

BARLEY (bär′lē) Barley is a widely used cereal plant of the genus *Hordeum*. This genus, having sixteen species, is a member of the grass family. Barleys are found in Europe, Asia, northern Africa, and North America. Barley heads usually have long, bristly flowers that grow in tightly bunched spikes, with three additional spikes at each node. (*See* NODE.) Most barleys are considered weeds by people. One species, called squirrel tail grass, is grown for use as an ornament. Barley grown as a crop comes from three species, with two, four, or six rows of grain on the spike. Such barley is used as animal feed, to make malt for use in such products as beer and malted milk, as an ingredient in soups, and to make flour for use in cereal and bread.

Barley thrives in cool climates. In warmer climates, barley is planted as a winter crop. Spring barley is planted in spring and matures by summer. Winter barley is planted in fall and harvested the next summer. The grain should be harvested when it is dry enough so that a kernel snaps when bitten. Barley can be grown in the same place for many years if the soil is properly fed and if the barley does not succumb to diseases or soil erosion. The world produces about 7,120,000,000 bushels of barley a year. The Soviet Union is the largest producer.   J.J.A./F.W.S.

BARNACLE (bär′ni kəl) Barnacles are saltwater crustaceans that spend their entire adult lives attached to underwater objects. (*See* CRUSTACEAN.) Barnacles have been found on rocks, turtles, whales, buoys, and ship bottoms. There are about eight hundred species of barnacles. Most grow a hard, stony covering around themselves for protection. This covering has an opening for the barnacle's legs. Barnacles capture microscopic organisms for food by waving their legs out this

Barnacles are saltwater crustaceans that usually grow a hard, strong covering around themselves for protection. They spend their lives attached to underwater objects.

opening. The motion of their legs also brings dissolved oxygen into the shell. When in danger, the barnacle pulls its legs inside the shell and hides.

Barnacles have three life stages. In the first, they are small, free-swimming creatures with one eye. In the second stage, they have six pairs of legs, two eyes, and two feelers. In the third stage, they still have twelve legs, but they lose their eyes. They attach themselves to underwater objects during this stage.

Barnacles that attach themselves to the bottoms of ships cause serious problems. They slow the ships by increasing the ships' resistance to the water. They also add weight. Barnacles may increase the weight of an ocean liner by several tons. This is known as the fouling problem.   A.J.C./C.S.H.

BARNARD, CHRISTIAAN NEETHLING

(1922-   ) Dr. Christiaan Barnard is a South African surgeon who performed the first human heart transplant operation. On December 3, 1967, he transplanted a heart into 55-year-old Louis Washkansky. The heart had belonged to a 25-year-old woman who had died in an automobile accident. Washkansky lived for eighteen days but finally died of a lung infection. Barnard has since performed many such operations. In 1974, he transplanted a human heart into a patient without removing the patient's own heart. He joined the donor heart to the patient's heart, providing a "double pump" for the circulatory system. Barnard also experimented with transplanting animal hearts into human beings. *See also* HEART; TRANSPLANTATION.   A.J.C./D.G.F.

BAROMETER (bə räm′ət ər) A barometer is

a device that measures atmospheric, or air, pressure. It is used to help forecast the weather

and to measure the altitude, or height, of objects and areas above sea level.

In 1643, an Italian, Evangelista Torricelli, showed that when a tube sealed at one end was filled with mercury and turned upside down into a bowl of mercury, the mercury in

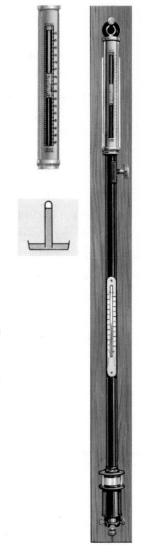

The Fortin mercury barometer is shown on the far right. This instrument consists of a glass tube, open at one end, that is filled with mercury. When the tube is turned upside down and immersed in a container of mercury (small bottom drawing), the mercury in the tube falls only a short distance because the air pressure on the surface of the mercury in the container holds the mercury column up. The top part of the tube has very little air—it is a partial vacuum. Changes in outside air pressure cause the height of the mercury column to rise or fall. The height is measured in inches or in millimeters, using the brass scale (small top drawing) that slides up and down the barometer.

the tube fell until its top was at a certain height. The weight of air pressing down on the mercury in the bowl held the mercury in the tube at that height. Torricelli was able to show that air pressure at sea level is normally 30 in. [76 cm], the height of mercury in a tube that has a diameter of 0.3937 in. [1 cm]. Other scientists then reasoned that altitude could be measured by observing changes in the height of the mercury at different locations. Because air is thinner at great heights, they believed its pressure would support less mercury as height increased. The higher above sea level, the lower the column of mercury would be. This was proven to be true. Today, barometers are used in airplanes to measure altitude. They are called altimeters. (*See* ALTIMETER.)

In a mercury barometer, a printed scale beside the tube containing mercury gives the barometric reading, or measurement. It may be written in inches or millimeters or in units called bars and millibars. In 1939, the United States Weather Bureau adopted the bar as a unit of measurement. It gives a more exact pressure reading at sea level of 29.53 in. [75.01 cm]. One millibar equals a column of mercury 0.03 in. [0.08 cm] high in a tube with a diameter of 0.39 in. [1 cm], or 1/1,000 of a bar.

A mercury barometer is used for weather forecasting. When the mercury drops rapidly, a storm is forecast. When the mercury rises steadily, good weather is forecast.

Aneroid barometers use no liquid. They show air pressure by recording its effect on an airtight box that has had some of its air taken out. The sides of the box move in and out according to the amount of air pressure on them. The movements of the sides are recorded by a pointer, which moves across a scale. Aneroid barometers are smaller than mercury barometers and easier to carry.

The barograph is an aneroid barometer that scientists use to keep records of changes in air pressure. The barograph records air pressure on paper that is attached to a revolving drum. *See also* ATMOSPHERE; ATMOSPHERE (UNIT); MILLIBAR; WEATHER.   H.G./E.W.L.; C.R.

BARRACUDA (bar′ə küd′ə) The barracuda is a saltwater fish belonging to the family Sphyraenidae. It is a long, slender fish with many large, sharp teeth. Barracuda are found in coastal waters of warm seas throughout the world. There are five species of barracuda in North American waters. The great barracuda, which lives off the coast of Florida, may reach lengths of 8 ft. [2.5 m]. Although the barracuda is considered dangerous by many skin divers, very few instances have been recorded of this fish attacking swimmers.   S.R.G./E.C.M.

BASALT (bə sôlt′)) Basalt is a heavy, black or gray igneous rock made of tiny grains. (*See* IGNEOUS ROCK.) The grains are crystals, usually made of the minerals plagioclase and pyroxene. Basalt is formed from lava, the red-hot liquid from volcanoes. Basalt is the most common volcanic rock. Hawaii, Samoa, and Tahiti are volcanic islands formed of basalt.

When lava cools and hardens to form basalt, the basalt can split in columns, resembling giant stepping stones on the surface. Cliffs having basalt columns are among famous tourist attractions. One is the Devil's Postpile in California; another is the Giant's Causeway in Northern Ireland. Some large basalt fields have been built by lava flowing from narrow openings in the ground. On the Columbia Plateau, a basalt field in the state of Washington, the basalt is about 3,300 ft. [1,000 m] or more thick.

Crushed basalt is used to make roads and as building stone. *See also* ROCK; VOLCANO.
     J.J.A./R.H.

BASE In chemistry, a base is often described as a compound that can combine with an acid to form a salt. Acids produce hydrogen ions (H^+) when they are dissolved in water or other solvents. Bases produce basic ions that combine with hydrogen ions. The most common basic ion is the hydroxal ion (OH)⁻. (*See* ACID; COMPOUND; IONS AND IONIZATION.)

Most bases contain atoms of a metal and one or more hydroxyl (OH⁻) groups. These bases are formed when a metal oxide reacts with water. (*See* OXIDATION AND REDUCTION.) Bases in water solution taste bitter and feel slippery. They turn red litmus paper blue. In a solution, bases ionize, or break down, into positive and negative ions. A strong base, such as sodium hydroxide (NaOH), breaks down almost completely in solution. (*See* SOLUTION AND SOLUBILITY.) Such bases are called alkalis. (*See* ALKALI.) A weak base, such as ammonium hydroxide (NH_4OH), ionizes (breaks down) only slightly in water. Bases have a pH from 7 to 14. The stronger the base, the higher the pH number.

The bases sodium hydroxide (caustic soda) and potassium hydroxide (caustic potash) are used in making soap, paper, bleach, and many kinds of chemicals. Along with ammonium hydroxide, or ammonia solution, they are useful cleaning agents because they cause reactions that remove grease. Calcium oxide (quicklime) is used to make glass, and calcium hydroxide (slaked lime) to make mortar. *See also* NEUTRALIZATION.   J.J.A./A.D.

BASIDIUM (bə sid′ē əm) The basidium is the reproductive structure in Basidiomycetes, an advanced class of fungi. Common varieties of these fungi are mushrooms and puffballs. Each fungus contains hundreds of the teardrop-shaped basidia (plural of *basidium*). Each basidium contains four spores. Once the spores are released, the fungus dies. Each spore may produce a new fungus. *See also* FUNGUS; MUSHROOM; SPORE.   A.J.C./M.J.C.; M.H.S.

BASKET STAR The basket star is a marine echinoderm. It is a member of the class Ophiuroidea. (*See* ECHINODERMATA.) The basket star gets its name from its star-shaped body and its five long arms. Each of these arms branches off into other arms, making this organism look like a basket. The arms are used to gather debris to be eaten as food. The basket star lives on the ocean floor. *See also* BRITTLE STAR.   A.J.C./C.S.H.

Basket stars are marine animals that are related to starfish. The basket star gets its name from its star-shaped body and its long arms.

BASS (bas) Bass is the name given to several kinds of fish. True basses are saltwater fishes belonging to the Percichythyidae and Serranidae families. Well-known examples are the striped bass, channel bass, and grouper.

Better known, however, are the freshwater basses. They belong to the sunfish family, Centrarchidae. The largemouth bass and smallmouth bass are especially popular game fishes. The fishes were originally found in only some areas in North America. They have since been taken to waters in every state and to many countries around the world. The world's record largemouth bass weighed 24 lb., 4 oz. [10.9 kg]. It was caught in the state of Georgia.

S.R.G./E.C.M.

BAT Bats are the only mammals that can fly. Their wings are actually long arms and fingers covered with a thin skin that connects down the body to the lower legs. Like other mammals, bats have legs, but they do not walk on them. They depend almost entirely on flying, using their legs and feet when they hang upside down in a roosting position.

Bats are furry animals that usually look somewhat like mice. They vary in size. The smallest have bodies 1.5 in. [3.8 cm] long with a wingspread of about 6 in. [15 cm]. The largest may be 12 in. [30 cm] long and have a wingspread of 6 ft. [1.8 m]. Some bats, depending on the shape and length of their wings, can fly as fast as 15 m.p.h. [24 kph].

Bats are flying mammals that navigate by sound waves. There are many species of bats, including the red bat (above) and the Mexican free-tailed bat (below).

The smaller ones fly around 5 to 8 m.p.h. [8 to 13 kph].

Bats have nocturnal habits, sleeping during the day and flying at night in search of food. They live together in colonies and roost in trees and caves. Many species feed on insects. By eating insects that people consider pests, bats are beneficial to humankind.

A very interesting part of bat behavior is how they navigate at night in search of food. They have very poor vision and cannot see well in the dark. They fly and locate food using a system called echolocation. They send out very high sounds in the form of short bursts. The sounds are too high-pitched for human beings to hear. The sounds bounce off objects and return as echoes, helping the animals determine the direction and distance of anything in their paths. Bats can detect and catch insects in the air. Experiments in the laboratory show they are even able to locate and avoid hitting very fine wires strung in their way. This system of echolocation is similar to, and in fact helped lead to the development of, the sonar and radar systems developed by people for navigation under the sea and in the air.

Bats usually mate in the fall. The young are born in the spring. The females may have from one to four babies a year, depending on the kind of bat. Because bats do not build nests, infant bats must cling to their mothers for several weeks. During this time, the young are given thorough training in flying and hunting.

There are many species of bats living all over the world. The most common kinds to be found in North America are the brown bats, the Mexican free-tailed bats, the hoary bats, and the silver-haired bats.

A common kind found in Central and South America is the vampire bat. It is known especially for its unique habit of feeding on the blood of other animals, mainly cattle. The vampire bat digs into the skin of its prey with sharp bites, then licks the blood from the wound. The vampire bat drinks about 42 oz. [15 ml] of blood each day. However, vampire bats are dangerous to people and animals only if they carry the disease rabies.   P.G.C./J.J.M.

BATHOLITH (bath′ə lith′) A batholith is a huge body of rock formed by the forcing and hardening of material moving upward from the earth's interior into the crust. The surface of a batholith is usually more than 40 sq. mi. [100 sq. km]. It may be much larger. Masses covering less than 40 sq. mi. are called stocks.

Forced up from the earth's interior, batholiths are dome-shaped structures. They were once thought to have unknown depth. Recent studies show that many of them have floors with a thickness of at least 3,300 ft. [1,000 m]. Rocks lying on top of a batholith may be forced upward into an arch. Batholiths are seen only when the overlying rocks have been worn away.   J.J.A./W.R.S.

BATHYSPHERE AND BATHYSCAPHE A bathysphere (bath′i sfir′) is a hollow steel ball with portholes, once used for deep-sea exploring. It is large enough to hold one person inside. The bathysphere was designed by Otis Barton, an American. It was used in the 1930s and 1940s to go down as far as 3,300 ft. [1,000 m] under the sea. The bathysphere, attached to a ship by a cable, was always being knocked around as the ship was tossed about on the waves.

The bathyscaphe (bath′i skaf′) was designed to overcome this problem. It was invented by Auguste Piccard, a Swiss scientist, who was famous for his balloon flights.

(*See* PICCARD, AUGUSTE.) The bathyscaphe is free-floating. It is supported by a large float tank filled with gasoline. Piccard started work in 1939. In 1948, he dived in his bathyscaphe *FNRS* to a depth of more than 5,000 ft. [1,524 m]. His later, improved bathyscaphe, *Trieste*, was bought by the United States Navy. The *Trieste* went down 35,800 ft. [10,912 m] into the Mariana Trench in the Pacific in 1960.

Research and development programs for deep-diving vehicles have continued. Their goals are related to national defense, the need for services such as search and rescue, salvage operations, and the promise of new resources from the ocean.   J.J.A./R.W.L.

PROJECT

BATTERY (bat′ə rē) A battery is a device that produces electricity by chemical action. A battery contains one or more units called cells. Each cell can produce electric current. Single cell batteries are used to power flashlights and toys. Batteries with several cells provide electricity for automobiles, heavy equipment, spacecraft, submarines, and emergency electric lights.

The first battery was developed in the late 1790s by Count Alessandro Volta, an Italian scientist. (*See* VOLTA, ALESSANDRO.) In 1859, a French physicist, Gaston Plante, invented the first lead-acid storage battery. Another French scientist, George Leclanche, introduced the first dry cell battery a few years later.

Primary, or dry cell, batteries do not have long lives. They stop giving off electricity when their chemicals lose their power. These batteries usually consist of one cell. Secondary, or wet cell, batteries can be used for years. They can be recharged many times after they are first discharged. They usually consist of several cells.

Batteries come in many sizes. Tiny ones used to power electric watches and hearing aids weigh as little 0.05 oz. [1.4 g]. Huge batteries used in submarines weigh up to 1 ton [0.91 metric ton]. The average automobile storage battery weighs about 35 to 40 lb. [16 to 18 kg].

Batteries differ in voltages, or power. A typical flashlight battery produces 1½ volts.

Dry cell batteries Millions of dry cell batteries are manufactured each year. They contain rodlike structures called electrodes. A thick, pastelike chemical substance that can conduct electricity, called an electrolyte, surrounds the electrodes. (*See* ELECTRODE.) The

Although batteries come in many different shapes and sizes, they are all designed for one task—producing electricity by chemical action.

zinc casings of dry cells also act as electrodes. Chemical reaction between the electrolyte and the electrodes creates an electric charge, or voltage difference, between the electrodes. When a device is attached to the electrodes, the current flows from one electrode to the other, making the device work.

There are three main types of dry cell batteries: carbon-zinc, alkaline, and mercury. The carbon-zinc battery was developed first. Most flashlight batteries are of the carbon-zinc type. The rodlike electrode is made of carbon. The other electrode is the zinc casing. The electrolyte consists of ammonium chloride, zinc chloride, and water. Carbon-zinc batteries can be recharged. However, the charge only lasts a short time.

An alkaline dry cell battery is more powerful. It lasts five to eight times longer than a carbon-zinc battery. It has a carbon electrode and a zinc casing electrode. The electrolyte is a strong alkali solution, potassium hydroxide. (*See* ALKALI.) Alkaline dry cells are used mainly for portable radios.

In a mercury dry cell, the voltage remains constant to the end of the battery's life. A mercuric oxide electrode is used. The other electrode is the zinc casing. The electrolyte is potassium hydroxide.

Wet cell batteries Wet cell, or storage, batteries produce much more electricity than dry cell batteries. They are large in size and can be recharged many times. There are two main types of storage batteries: lead-acid and nickel-cadmium.

Lead-acid batteries consist of plastic or hard rubber containers with three or six cells. Each cell contains two sets of electrodes. One set is positive. The other set is negative. The electrolyte is a mixture of sulfuric acid and water. Chemical reaction causes an electric charge to build up at the electrodes. Each cell generates two volts of electricity. Most automobile storage batteries contain six cells that generate a total of twelve volts. Such a battery is charged by passing electricity through it. When in operation, electrons flow from the negative pole to the positive pole. A recent development in lead-acid batteries is the maintenance-free battery. It does not require the periodic addition of water. It lasts longer because its electrodes are made of alloys containing lead, calcium, and tin. Unlike the electrodes in regular lead-acid batteries, these electrodes do not cause the battery to discharge, or lose its power, when it is not in use.

Nickel-cadmium storage batteries operate on the same general principles as lead-acid batteries but contain a different electrolyte and different electrodes. The electrolyte is a solution of potassium hydroxide. The positive electrodes are made of nickel oxide, and the negative electrodes are made of cadmium. Nickel-cadmium batteries can be sealed airtight. They do not require periodic additions of water. This makes them ideal for use in portable tools and equipment and in space satellites. *See also* ELECTRICITY; FUEL CELL.

W.R.P./L.L.R.

BAUD (bȯd) Baud is a measure of the speed per second at which an electronic signal travels between computers. One baud is equal to the transmission of one bit per second. *Bit* refers to a unit of information. As the baud rate increases, communication occurs faster. Personal computers can transmit information at a rate of 300 to 2,400 baud. More advanced systems can transmit information at rates of 9,600 baud. *See also* COMPUTER.

P.Q.F./L.W.

Bauxite being mined in the West Indies is shown at left. Bauxite is the ore that is the source of aluminum.

BAUXITE (bȯk′sīt′) Bauxite is the ore from which aluminum, the most abundant metal in the earth's crust, is extracted. (*See* ORE.) Bauxite is white, unless it has been stained red or brown by iron. Most bauxite is hard and rocklike, but some is soft like clay.

Bauxite is usually found in areas where the climate is hot and moist. For example, large deposits of bauxite are found in Arkansas, Alabama, and Georgia. Bauxite is also used to make alum, a white mineral salt found in some baking powders and cosmetics. Bauxite also may be mixed with clay to make bricks. These bricks line furnaces that melt steel. Bauxite is also combined with sulfuric acid to make aluminum sulfate, a chemical used in the paper, textile, and dye industries. *See also* ALUM; ALUMINUM. P.W./L.W.

BAYBERRY The bayberry is a West Indian tree. Its leaves produce bay oil. Bay oil is used in making perfumes and bay rum. This tree is also called the wild cinnamon tree.

The name *bayberry* is also given to a shrub found along the North American seacoasts. Its bark can be used to make a liquid that is used in medicine. A.J.C./M.H.S.

BEADLE, GEORGE WELLS (1903-1989) George Wells Beadle was an American scientist who worked in the field of genetics. In 1958, he and his co-worker, Edward L. Tatum, won the Nobel Prize for medicine for discoveries that helped explain how genes work. Beadle used a form of bread mold. By using X rays on the mold, he was able to show that irradiated genes have different chemical changes in their enzymes from genes that have not been irradiated. His experiments proved that genes control the making of enzymes. *See also* ENZYME; GENE; GENETICS; IRRADIATION. P.G.C./D.G.F.

BEAN The bean plant is a member of the pea family. (*See* PEA FAMILY.) Several different types of beans are grown widely for human use or animal feed. Beans vary in size, color, and tenderness.

The most important type of bean grown in the United States is the soybean. Other types include the scarlet runner bean and the kidney bean. The lima bean is grown mainly in Central America and the midwestern United States.

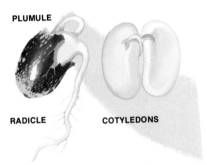

PLUMULE

RADICLE   COTYLEDONS

The runner bean seed is shown germinating, or sprouting, (above left) and spilt open (above right). The runner bean has large, fleshy cotyledons (seed leaves), a small radicle (young root), and a plumule (young shoot).

The bean plant grows as a shrub or as a tall climbing vine. Before the beans are ready to be picked, the plant usually has brightly colored flowers. The bean plant grows best in warm, moist climates.   A.J.C./J.R.

BEAR Bears belong to the family Ursidae. They are the largest carnivores (meat eaters) on land. Most bears live north of the equator. No wild bears live in Antarctica, Africa, or Australia. Although they are adapted for eating meat, most bears also eat plants. Bears have large, heavy, fur-covered bodies and short, strong legs. Each paw has five toes. Each of these toes ends in a long, heavy claw. These claws are always exposed and are used for feeding, digging, and fighting. The bottoms of the paws are hairless. Bears range in size from the sun bear at 66 lb. [30 kg] to the Alaskan brown bear at 1,700 lb. [780 kg].

Bears have small, weak eyes. Although their hearing is good, they rely almost entirely on their sense of smell. Bears have forty-two teeth. Some are for tearing meat, and others are for chewing it. All bears, even tame ones, are very protective. They often will attack any person or animal that threatens them, their food, their homes, or their cubs. Bears are able to run and swim quickly.

In spite of what many people think, bears do not hibernate. (*See* HIBERNATION.) Before the winter, they gain weight and find a cave or other suitable shelter. They sleep fitfully during the winter months. They may even wake up and wander around on warm days. Bears usually live alone. They never travel in groups. A male bear will stay with a female for about a month. Shortly after mating, the male leaves. The female is then left alone to find shelter for herself and her unborn cubs. Two cubs are usually born during the winter. Some females may give birth to as many as four cubs. The cubs are born hairless and weigh less than 1 lb. [0.5 kg]. They stay with the mother for two years. During this time, the mother teaches them to hunt and to care for themselves.   A.J.C./J.J.M.

Bears are the largest meat-eating animals that live on dry land. A brown bear is pictured.

BEARING (ber'ing) A bearing is the part of a machine that supports a moving part, reducing the friction, or rubbing, as much as possible. Bearings are made from a metal that is softer than that of the moving part. Bearings wear out faster than the moving parts but are easier to replace. Many bearings are lined with a soft metal called Babbitt metal.

The most common types of bearings are the ball and roller bearings. These bearings depend on the principle that rolling produces much less friction than sliding. The revolving pivot, or journal, inside a ball bearing works upon a number of smaller steel balls. The balls roll easily in a track called the race. These balls are in a frame that keeps them apart from each other but allows contact with the moving parts of the machine. Roller bearings are similar but have rollers shaped like cylinders or tapered cones instead of balls. The rollers usually lie side by side around the shaft.

Ball bearings are widely used for decreasing friction in machines. Steel balls roll along a circular track inside the bearing.

A plain, or oil-film, bearing consists of a soft metal shell. A plain bearing is often called a sleeve bearing, because it fits around a shaft within a machine like a coat sleeve. A film of oil covers both the bearing and the shaft to help reduce friction. The bearing is usually made of Babbitt metal, but copper and lead alloys are also widely used. Nylon bearings are used for much lighter load work. Friction between plastics and metal is quite low, and water can be used as a lubricant.

Some machines, such as refrigerator motors, use self-lubricating bearings because the machine cannot be lubricated after assembly. The jewel bearing, used in some watches and airplane instruments, has a pivot often made of crystal or a gemstone, such as ruby.

J.J.A./R.W.L.

BEATS Beats are regular variations in the loudness of a sound. (*See* SOUND.) Beats occur when two sound waves of almost the same pitch overlap. The pitch of a sound is controlled by its frequency. Suppose that two sounds have frequencies of 440 hertz (cycles per second) and 442 hertz. If the waves overlap, they combine to form a sound whose frequency is midway between the two. Its frequency is 441 hertz. The loudness of this sound increases and decreases. The number of beats you hear is equal to the difference in the frequencies of the two sounds. In this case, there are two beats per second.

Beats are caused by interference between the two sound waves. When the two waves reinforce each other, they make a loud sound. When they cancel each other out, the sound is soft. The same thing sometimes happens between two light waves. They can interfere to produce patterns of light and dark. This is also a form of beats. *See also* HERTZ.　M.E./J.T.

THE BEAUFORT SCALE FOR WIND CLASSIFICATION			
Beaufort Number	Speed (m.p.h.)	Description	Effects
0	0-1	Calm	Smoke rises vertically
1	1-3	Light air	Wind direction shown by drift of smoke
2	4-7	Slight breeze	Wind felt on face; leaves rustle; wind vanes moved
3	8-12	Gentle breeze	Leaves and twigs in constant motion; light flags extended
4	13-18	Moderate breeze	Dust and small branches move; flags flap
5	19-24	Fresh breeze	Small trees sway; small waves on lakes and streams
6	25-31	Strong breeze	Large branches move; hard to use umbrellas
7	32-38	Moderate gale	Large trees sway
8	39-46	Fresh gale	Twigs break off trees; walking becomes difficult
9	47-54	Strong gale	Slight damage to houses (shingles removed)
10	55-63	Whole gale	Trees uprooted; much damage to houses
11	64-75	Storm	Widespread damage
12	over 75	Hurricane	Violent conditions; sometimes loss of life

The Beaufort number used to describe the wind tells more than the approximate speed of the air mass. It also briefly indicates the effects that can be expected from each particular wind condition.

BEAUFORT SCALE The Beaufort (bō′fərt) scale is a system of describing the speed of winds based on observations. Rear Admiral Sir Francis Beaufort of the British navy created the scale in 1805. It was originally used at sea but has been changed so that it may now be used on land as well. A person can learn the approximate speed of the wind from the scale by noticing the wind's effects. For example, a wind that begins to break twigs off of trees is a fresh gale with the Beaufort number 8. A more exact, objective measure of wind speed is now found by using instruments. *See also* ANEMOMETER. S.R.G./C.R.

BEAVER (bē′vər) The beaver is a rodent with a large, thickset body and short, strong legs. (*See* RODENT.) The beaver's hind feet are webbed for swimming. The forefeet do not have webs. The beaver uses its forefeet almost like hands. Its tail is broad and flat like a paddle and is of great use in swimming. The beaver's body can reach a length of 3 ft. [90 cm] and can weigh as much as 60 lb. [27 kg].

Beavers are aquatic animals. They live in and around lakes and streams and are common in the northern United States and in Canada. Observers of the behavior of the beaver are impressed with the animal's ability to build dams, lodges, and canals. Beavers have been called the engineers of the animal kingdom.

Beavers build dams across creeks, ditches, and streams to form artificial ponds. They build their homes, called lodges, in these ponds. If the stream is quiet, they build the dam straight across it. If the stream has a strong current, they bow the dam in an inward curve so it can stand the pressure of the water.

Dams are built out of parts of trees cut down by the beavers with their sharp teeth. The animals float logs, limbs, and twigs of the

Beavers live in lodges (left) that they build of logs and branches that they gather (below right). They construct dams across streams, ditches, and creeks and then build the lodges, such as the one at left below, in the ponds that the dams create.

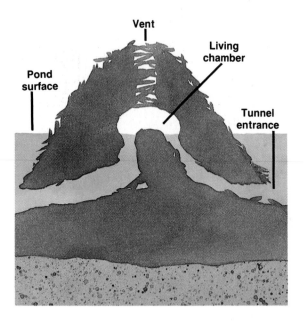

Vent

Living chamber

Pond surface

Tunnel entrance

trees into place where the dam is to be built. They interweave the limbs and twigs together and cover the structure with a mortar of clay and dead leaves. Beavers start their dams during the summer months when the level of the water is lowest. They continue construction until the first cold weather. They constantly repair the dams.

The lodges are built on the banks of the lake, in shallow areas in ponds, or on small islands. They look like large mud heaps but are constructed just like the dams. The beavers enter the inside of the lodge through a tunnel that comes up from below the level of the water. They use a second tunnel to bring in food for the winter.

In a Canadian national park, during a period of fifteen months, two beavers cut down 226 trees; built 3 dams, each 50 ft. [15 m] wide, across a river; constructed a lodge of 1,000 cu. ft. [28 cu. m]; and stored up bark, roots, and twigs for winter food in a pile of 720 cu. ft. [20 cu. m].

Beavers live together in families. The females have litters of two to four kits that stay with the families until they are two years old. They then go out to mate and start families of their own.

At one time, millions of beavers lived in North America. They were hunted for their valuable fur until laws were passed to protect them. Now, because they are protected, the number of beavers has greatly increased in some parts of the United States.   P.G.C./J.J.M.

BECQUEREL, ANTOINE HENRI (1852-1908)

Henri Becquerel was a French physicist who discovered radioactivity. Becquerel's grandfather had made several important discoveries in electrochemistry. His father worked with fluorescence and phosphorescence. Becquerel also worked with fluorescent substances, trying to find out if they gave off X rays. At one time, he accidentally placed some crystals of the mineral pitchblende next to some photographic film in a drawer. Later, he noticed that rays affecting the film were coming from an element in the pitchblende. This radioactive element was uranium. Becquerel showed his discovery to Marie Curie, who called the occurrence "radio activity." This led Curie to the discovery of radium, another radioactive element found in pitchblende. In 1903, Becquerel shared with Marie Curie and her husband Pierre the Nobel Prize physics. *See also* CURIE FAMILY; RADIO-ACTIVITY.   J.J.A./D.G.F.

BEDBUG Bedbugs are small insects that feed on the blood of humans and other animals. The bedbug pierces the skin of its victim with its sharp beak. Then it sucks up blood. Some humans suffer swelling and itching from the bites of bedbugs.(*See* PARASITE.)

The bedbug is a parasite that is active at night. During the day, it hides in bedding, furniture, walls, and floors.

Bedbugs are about 0.25 in. [6 mm] long and reddish brown. They have wings that are too small for flying. They usually come out at night. During the day they hide in bedding, furniture, cracks in the wall, or under the floor. The adult bedbug lays between 100 and 250 eggs. The eggs hatch in about two weeks. Bedbugs live as long as a year. The insects can be controlled with insecticides.

G.M.B./J.R.

BEDROCK (bed'räk) Bedrock is the solid rocky layer of the earth's crust that lies just below the surface. The upper part of the crust is mainly sedimentary rocks. Igneous and metamorphic rocks are found just under the sedimentary rocks. (*See* ROCK.) Igneous and metamorphic rocks form the solid bedrock. Movements within the earth can force bedrock above the sedimentary layer. Bedrock underlies the surface of some mountains. (*See* MOUNTAIN.) Mountainous areas can also have bedrock exposed at the surface. A section of exposed bedrock is called outcrop. *See also* EARTH.   P.W./L.W.

A honeybee collects nectar and pollen from a flower. Bees produce honey from the nectar, and they fertilize various plants as they carry the pollen from flower to flower.

BEE Bees are insects that belong to the order Hymenoptera. They are related to ants and wasps. There are many species of bees found all over the world. The body of a bee, which is seldom longer than 1.5 in. [3.75 cm], has three parts: a head, a thorax, and an abdomen. (*See* ABDOMEN; THORAX.) Two pairs of wings are attached to the thorax. Female bees have an organ called an ovipositor at the end of their abdomen. They use the ovipositor to lay eggs and to sting enemies.

Bees collect a sugary solution called nectar from flowers. They produce honey from the nectar. Honey is their major source of food. While the bee is collecting the nectar, it carries pollen from one flower to another. This results in pollination of the flower. Pollination is part of sexual reproduction in plants, so bees help perform a necessary task in nature. (*See* POLLINATION.)

Hatching bees undergo a metamorphosis, or series of changes. (*See* METAMORPHOSIS.) A larva hatches and turns into a pupa, which changes into an adult bee. The larva, pupa, and adult all look different.

There are solitary bees and social bees. There are many more kinds of solitary bees than there are kinds of social bees. Most solitary bees live alone. When they do live together, they do not divide up the work in the hive as social bees do. Some solitary bees, like the carpenter bee, make their nests in wood. Most build their nests underground. Each female solitary bee builds her own nest. It has many cells, or holes, in it. The bee puts honey and nectar in the cells and then lays an egg in each one. After covering the cells, she leaves to build other nests. The honey in the cells provides food for the young bees that hatch from the eggs.

Social bees live together in large numbers. Their nests are called hives. Some social bees, like the honeybee, build their hives in dead trees. Social bees divide up their work. Different kinds of bees do different kinds of jobs.

Bumblebees One of the better-known social bees is the bumblebee. It belongs to the family Apidae. It has a thick, hairy body, sometimes reaching 1.5 in. [3.75 cm] in length. It is colored with yellow and black stripes. A queen bumblebee moves into holes or abandoned animal nests in the spring and prepares a cell from the wax within her body. She then collects some pollen, puts it in the cell, and deposits her eggs on it. Like a bird, she sits on the eggs, protecting them from the chill of the early spring weather. The eggs hatch into worker bees who take over the building and enlarging of the nest. The worker bees are female bees unable to mate with males. The colony grows until there are a few hundred bees, but some colonies contain up to two thousand bees. Toward the end of the summer, the queen lays eggs that hatch into males and queen bees. The new queen bees mate with

A honeybee emerges after having undergone a complete metamorphosis from egg to adult.

the males. A few weeks later, all the bees die except the queen bees. They hibernate for the winter and start building new nests in the spring.

Honeybees Another social bee is the honeybee, which also belongs to the family Apidae. This bee's body is dark brown with yellow bands. The honeybee is about 0.5 in. [1.2 cm] long. Honeybees build their hives in tree hollows or in cracks in the walls of barns.

There is usually a lot of activity around the hives of honeybees. When the food supply is low, many bees must go out to gather a new supply. When food is plentiful, some of the bees remain behind. They continually inspect their hives to make sure everything is in order. They make sure that it is kept in good repair. Bees returning with pollen and nectar let the other bees know where to find the food supply by doing special dancelike movements. The movements show how far away and in what direction from the hive the food can be found.

Domesticated honeybees, kept for production of honey, are called domestic bees. They are kept in wooden hives, which can be enlarged as the colony grows. Beekeepers remove honey from the hives during the summer, being careful to leave enough so that the bees can survive the winter.

Social classes among honeybees The honeybee society has three main divisions: the workers, who provide food and protection for the colony; the queen, who lays the eggs; and the drones, who mate with the queen. An average honeybee hive contains one queen, one hundred drones, and sixty thousand workers.

The workers are female bees. They are the smallest bees in the hive. They can lay eggs but cannot mate, so the eggs are never fertilized. Each worker has a barbed stinger at the back end of the abdomen. When a bee stings another insect, it can withdraw its stinger without harm to itself. However, when a bee stings a human or other large animal, the barbs on the stinger stick under the animal's skin. A part of the bee's abdomen is pulled off when the bee tries to withdraw its stinger. The bee then dies.

For the first two weeks of a worker's adult life, she acts as a nurse. She feeds the queen, the drones, and the larvae. From the sixth day to the fourteenth day of her life, she secretes a substance called royal jelly from her mouth. Royal jelly is used to feed the larvae. When the worker is fourteen days old, she begins to produce wax from glands on the underside of her abdomen. She uses this wax to build the cells that form the structure called the honeycomb. When a worker is three weeks old, she joins in the search for pollen and nectar. She also cleans the hive and stands guard at the hive's entrance.

Worker bees collect pollen from flowers and carry it in their sacs, or leg baskets. These sacs are rows of small spines on their rear legs. A single bee can collect balls of pollen as large as 0.25 in. [6.3 mm] in diameter. The pollen is mixed with the bees' saliva to make a substance called beebread, used for food.

Nectar is also collected by the workers. They carry it in a special stomach in their bodies called the crop or honey sac. A bee must visit about one thousand flowers to fill its honey sac. It takes sixty full honey sacs to provide enough honey to fill a thimble. Honey is deposited in the honeycomb to ripen and thicken before each cell of the comb is sealed.

Workers use propolis, a resin from trees, to block up holes in their hives. They also use it to seal off the bodies of small animals who get into the hive and are stung to death.

Water is collected by the workers to dilute honey that has become too thick. It is also used to keep the hive moist and cool in hot weather.

Workers that are hatched in the spring or summer live from four to six weeks. Those that hatch in the fall live until the following spring.

A bee is an advanced insect that goes through complete metamorphosis. The first stage after the egg is the larva, or grub (left). During the pupal stage (middle), many changes take place, preparing the way for the adult form (right).

The queen bee is nearly twice as large as the other bees. She usually lives from four to five years. Her function is to produce eggs so that the colony can continue. She may lay up to three thousand eggs in one day. When a queen dies, the workers prepare queen cells for the last eggs that were laid. These cells are larger than other cells and are oblong rather than six-sided. Sometimes they are made while a queen is still alive. Eggs are placed in the queen cells, and they hatch into larvae. The larvae are fed royal jelly for a longer period than the usual three days. This makes them develop into queen bees rather than into worker bees. When a queen comes out of her cell, she immediately seeks out and kills any other queen larvae in the hive. Should there be another adult queen present, the two will fight until one of them kills the other. A queen bee never stings any bee except another queen. If she is prevented from killing a rival queen, one of them will leave the hive. She takes two thousand to twenty thousand bees along with her to start a new colony.

Drones are male bees born from unfertilized eggs laid by female workers. (*See* PARTHENOGENESIS.) Drones are larger than workers but smaller than queens. Drones do not have stingers. Their tongues are not long enough for them to obtain nectar. That is why they must be fed by the workers.

The main function of the drones is to mate with the queen so that she can lay fertilized eggs. The queen and a drone fly out of the hive and mate in the air.

During the summer, about one hundred drones are permitted to live in the hive and be fed. If other drones appear, they are killed. When food becomes scarce in the fall, the drones in the colony are stung to death and removed from the hive. S.R.G./J.R.

BEECH FAMILY The beech family has about four hundred species of trees, including the chestnut and oak. These trees grow to a height of 120 ft. [36.5 m]. Beeches are monoecious, which means that both male and female flowers grow on the same plant. The rounded male flowers are on thin stalks. The female flowers grow in pairs or in groups of three.

Beeches are deciduous, shedding their thin leaves once every year. (*See* DECIDUOUS TREE.) The leaves are sometimes colored red or purple. The fruit of these trees, called mast, is an important food for animals. Beechwood is used for furniture, flooring, fuel, and as pulp in making paper. J.J.A./M.H.

BEETLE (bēt′l) Beetles are insects belonging to the order Coleoptera. There are at least 278,000 kinds of beetles. Four of every ten insects are beetles.

Beetles are most easily identified by their elytra, a pair of hard shields that often cover the wings and most of the body. Beetles, which have strong jaws for biting, feed on plants and animals.

All insects have three-part bodies, made up of the head, the thorax, and the abdomen. (*See* ABDOMEN; THORAX.) However, unlike the bodies of other insects, the sections of the bodies of beetles are closely and strongly joined. Beetles are many different colors. Some are brightly colored. Others are dull. Beetles develop from eggs to larvae to pupae to adults. (*See* METAMORPHOSIS.) Most live for

The many thousands of types of beetles are found in almost every environment. This particular type, called the milkweed beetle, prefers to live on milkweed plants.

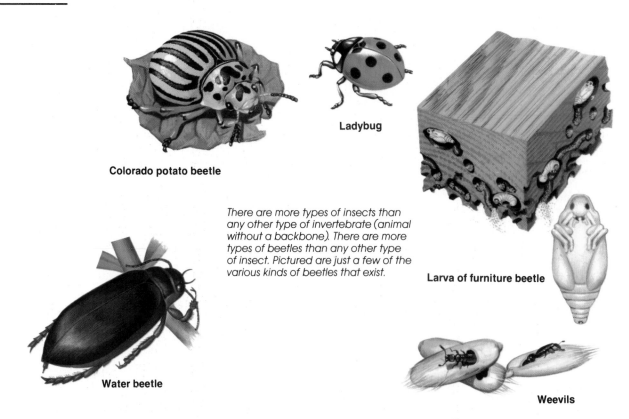

Colorado potato beetle

Ladybug

There are more types of insects than any other type of invertebrate (animal without a backbone). There are more types of beetles than any other type of insect. Pictured are just a few of the various kinds of beetles that exist.

Larva of furniture beetle

Water beetle

Weevils

about one year. A few live for up to five years. Some may live for only a few weeks. Beetles may live in water, or above or under the ground. Some beetles eat meat, while others eat plants. Beetles such as the ladybug are helpful to plant life. They eat smaller insects, such as aphids, that are harmful to plants.

Some beetles are too small to be seen with the naked eye. The largest beetle is the African Goliath beetle, which is the largest insect. Goliath beetles can grow to be 4 in. [10 cm] long and 8 in. [20 cm] wide.

The June beetle, or June bug, is common in the United States. It is a large, brown insect that can be seen on plants in the spring. The Japanese beetle is also common in the United States. It was brought from Asia to North America in 1916. Like the June beetle, it is a plant eater that is considered a pest.

G.M.B./J.R.

BEGONIA (bi gōn′yə) The begonia is a plant with waxy leaves and brightly colored flowers. It grows mainly in tropical climates as a vine and shrub. The species cultivated in the United States is usually small. The blossoms may grow as single or double flowers, and their colors may be red, orange, yellow, white, or pink. Begonia leaves are smooth and shiny with a waxy covering.

The root of the begonia can be tuberous or fibrous. Begonias with tuberous roots have large flowers and bloom in the summer. The fibrous types are used as houseplants and bloom in the winter. Many types, such as the rex begonia, have few flowers but are grown for their colorful leaves. *See also* ROOT; TUBER.

P.G.C./M.H.S.

BEHAVIOR OF ANIMALS Every species of animal acts differently. Each eats a certain food. Each lives in a certain place. Each reproduces in a certain way. The ways an animal acts are the behavior of the animal. Scientists who study animal behavior are called ethologists.

There are two main types of animal behavior: instinctive and learned. Instinctive behavior is behavior that the animal inherits from its parents. (*See* HEREDITY; INSTINCT.) A young fish does not have to learn how to swim. It knows how to swim right after it is born. Learned behavior is behavior that has to be taught to the animal. For example, a human child does not know how to tie a shoe until he or she is taught to do so.

Instinctive behavior An ethologist can find out which behavior is learned by taking a very young animal away from all other members of its species. The animal's subsequent behavior will be instinctive because there is no other animal to teach it. If a bird that is hatched away from all other birds can fly, then flying is instinctive behavior. Most of the courtship and mating behavior by which an animal reproduces is instinctive. Instinctive behavior is caused, or triggered, by a signal called a releaser. Releasers may be things that are seen, heard, smelled, felt, or tasted. The sight of a hawk overhead is a releaser for a mouse to run and hide. The releaser for an animal to eat is hunger.

An interesting example of instinctive behavior is found among a kind of fish known as the stickleback. A male stickleback instinctively chases other males out of his territory. If a male is chased into his own territory, he will turn, attack, and drive off the first stickleback. The releaser in this case seems to be the red belly of the male. A stickleback in his territory will attack even a dummy of the correct size and color. However, he will pay no attention to a male stickleback that has been painted to conceal his red belly.

Many animals that live in groups have developed instinctive behavior that controls the group. Examples of such social animals are insect colonies, schools of fish, herds of deer, and flocks of birds. Aggressive or unfriendly behavior does accur among animals. How-

Various animals, such as African antelopes, live in groups. The antelopes' behaviors within the group are instinctive behaviors.

ever, there is rarely an actual fight among members of the same species. It is even more rare for the animals to hurt or kill each other. For example, wolves may growl at each other. However, before a fight actually begins, the younger or smaller wolf backs away. This instinctive behavior prevents animals from killing or harming members of their own group.

Learned behavior This kind of behavior is learned from experience. A dog learns to avoid a busy highway. If a cat learns that mice live in a woodpile, the cat will visit the area often. Many animals are trained by humans. Seeing-eye dogs that help blind people get around are displaying learned behavior. There are many different kinds of learned behavior. One of the most interesting kinds was discovered by Konrad Lorenz, an Austrian ethologist. He learned that when a baby bird hatches from the egg, it identifies the first object it sees as its mother. He called this imprinting. When Lorenz artificially hatched goose eggs and stood next to the hatching eggs, the baby geese thought he was their mother. They followed him wherever he went.

Vertebrates have better-developed brains than invertebrates, so they are better able to learn behavior. Mammals generally learn faster than other kinds of vertebrates, and humans learn behavior faster than any other species. *See also* ANIMAL KINGDOM. S.R.G./R.J.B.

BEKESY, GEORG VON (1899-1972) Georg von Bekesy was a physicist and physiologist who is best known for his work on the way the ear receives sound. In 1961, he was awarded the Nobel Prize for physiology. He studied sound and the way it is analyzed and communicated to the brain by a part of the inner ear called the cochlea. Bekesy experimented with the ears of humans and animals, including an elephant. He constructed physical models that showed how sounds travel in the cochlea and along the basilar membrane of the ear. He worked at Harvard University and at the University of Hawaii. *See also* EAR.

P.G.C./D.G.F.

BELL, ALEXANDER GRAHAM (1847-1922) Alexander Graham Bell was a Scottish-American scientist who invented the telephone. Born in Scotland, Bell and his family moved to Ontario, Canada, for health reasons. Bell's two brothers had died of tuberculosis, and Bell himself was showing signs of the disease. Bell recovered within a year. At twenty-three years of age, Bell devoted himself to improving communication among the deaf.

Alexander Graham Bell

While experimenting with the possibility of sending several telegraph signals over one wire at the same time, Bell became interested in sending voice sounds over a wire. In 1874, Bell secured the help of Thomas Augustus Watson, an expert in the field of telegraphy. (*See* TELEGRAPH.) Watson was of great help in Bell's early experiments. Bell was issued a patent for the telephone in 1876. A year later, he founded the Bell Telephone Company.

In his later years, Bell continued working on new inventions. Some of his ideas led to the development of the iron lung, the radio, phonograph records, the hydrofoil, and the metal detector. His chief interest, though, remained the education of the deaf. He used much of his money and influence to establish research and care institutions in Europe and the United States. *See also* TELEPHONE.   A.J.C./D.G.F.

BENDS *See* CAISSON DISEASE.

BENTHOS (ben′thäs′) Benthos is the name for all organisms that live on or in the bottom of a body of water. Benthic organisms live on

Benthos *means "living at the bottom of the sea." These sea anemones are classified as benthic animals, even though they live in fairly shallow water.*

top of the sand beneath the ocean, under the mud beneath a lake, or among the rocks of a streambed. They can be plants, insects, worms, crustaceans, fishes, or other kinds of organisms. Many of the benthic animals eat dead matter that falls to the bottom from the water above. Benthic organisms are also a valuable source of food for other aquatic animals.

S.R.G./R.J.B.

BENZ, KARL (1844-1929) Born in Karlsruhe, Germany, Karl Benz was one of the first engineers to build motor-driven vehicles. He founded Benz and Company to manufacture gasoline engines. Benz started to build his first gas engine in 1879, building a practical automobile by 1885. He installed the gas engine on the back of a tricycle. The vehicle had an electric ignition, a water-cooled engine, shaped "poppet" valves, and a differential gear, features still common in automobiles today. A few months after Benz had finished his automobile, a fellow German, Gottlieb Daimler, completed a motorcycle powered by a gasoline engine. Karl Benz later designed a float-type carburetor and a transmission system. *See also* AUTOMOBILE.

J.J.A./D.G.F.

BENZENE (ben′zēn′) Benzene is a colorless liquid with a strong odor. Benzene was discovered by Michael Faraday in 1825. (*See* FARADAY, MICHAEL.) Benzene is used in the manufacture of many chemical products, such as synthetic detergent, aniline dye, nylon, synthetic rubber, and Styrofoam. (*See* ANILINE; NYLON; RUBBER.)

Benzene has the chemical formula C_6H_6. The benzene molecule has its carbon atoms arranged in a ring called a benzene ring. Benzene belongs to a group of compounds called

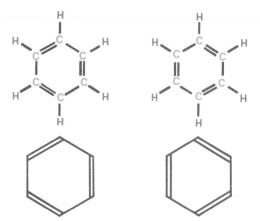

Ovens heat coal to a high temperature to produce coke. Coke is used in the making of iron and steel. This process releases poisonous benzene molecules into the atmosphere (above). The molecule of benzene has six carbon atoms and six hydrogen atoms joined in a ring by alternate single and double bonds. These bonds may be drawn in either of two arrangements (left and right, below), but usually are drawn without the C and H symbols (left and right, bottom).

aromatic hydrocarbons. (*See* HYDROCARBON.) Benzene melts at 42°F. [5.5°C] and boils at 176.2°F. [80.1°C]. Benzene is sometimes called benzol.

One method of producing benzene is by heating coal tar and condensing (changing to a liquid) the vapors from the tar. Coal tar is a thick, black, sticky liquid that is a by-product in the manufacture of coke (coal that has been heated to a high temperature without air). Today, large amounts of benzene are obtained from petroleum rather than coal tar.

Benzene is a dangerous chemical. It is known to affect the blood and can cause severe anemia and leukemia (a form of cancer). (*See* ANEMIA; CANCER.) Those who come in constant contact with it, such as those who work in rubber factories, may be at a severe health risk. Benzene and its derivatives are no longer used in high-school chemistry laboratories. J.J.A.; P.Q.F./E.W.L.; J.M.; J.E.P.

BERIBERI (ber′ē ber′ē) Beriberi is a disease that affects the nervous and circulatory systems. It is caused by a lack of thiamine (vitamin B_1) in the diet. Beriberi causes severe pain and weakness in the arms and legs. It may cause difficulties with balance and coordination; memory problems; and swelling of the body tissues, called edema. In advanced cases, coma, heart failure, and death can occur.

Beriberi was very common in China, Japan, and the Philippines through the nineteenth century. The people in these countries had a diet consisting largely of polished white rice. Polishing the rice removes the outer layer, which contains thiamine. (*See* RICE.)

In modern times, people who drink large amounts of alcohol usually have unbalanced diets, which may lead to beriberi. The disease can be treated with a diet of thiamine-rich foods such as unpolished cereal grains, peas, and liver. Injections of synthetic (human-made) thiamine are also effective. *See also* DIET; NUTRITION; VITAMIN. A.J.C./L.V.C; J.J.F.

BERKELIUM *See* ELEMENT.

BERNOULLI FAMILY Bernoulli was the family name of three Swiss mathematicians and physicists. There were two brothers, Jacques and Jean, and Jean's son, Daniel. Each served as professor at the University of Basel in Switzerland.

Jacques Bernoulli (1654-1705) made important discoveries in mathematics. He worked on finite series and their sums, on calculus, and on trigonometry. He developed new material in the theory of probability. The Bernoulli numbers used in this branch of mathematics are named after him.

Jean Bernoulli (1667-1748) was also a mathematician, working on calculus and complex numbers. He also worked in applied mathematics, with subjects such as astronomy, the tides, optics, and ships' sails.

Daniel Bernoulli (1700-1782) was the best known member of the family. He developed the science of hydrodynamics, which is the branch of physics dealing with the forces that fluids in motion exert. One of his discoveries is known as Bernoulli's effect. (*See* BERNOULLI'S EFFECT.) He also worked on differential equations, trigonometry, calculus, and probability theory. J.J.A./D.G.F.

BERNOULLI'S EFFECT As the speed of a fluid or gas increases, its pressure decreases. This is known as Bernoulli's (bər nü′lēz) effect. It was first described by Daniel Bernoulli in the 1700s. (*See* BERNOULLI FAMILY.) Although Bernoulli was referring to liquids flowing steadily at one level, the effect has many other applications.

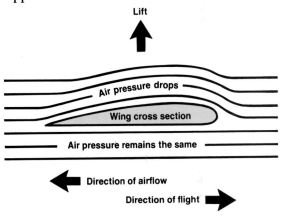

Bernoulli's effect in aerodynamics: Air moving over an airplane's wing goes a longer distance, so it must travel faster. Therefore, there is less air pressure on the top of the wing than on the bottom, which causes the wing to be pushed upward.

Bernoulli's effect allows airplanes to fly. An airplane wing, seen from the tip, is flat on the bottom and curved on the top. As the wing travels through the air, the air must travel either over or under the wing. Air moving over the wing goes a longer distance, so it must travel faster. Because air moving over the wing is moving faster, there is less air pressure on the top of the wing. This means that there is more pressure on the bottom of the wing, which pushes the wing upward, causing the plane to stay in the air.

The same effect can be seen in a bathroom shower. Water from the shower moves the air inside the shower faster than the air outside the shower. This means there is more air pressure on the outside of the shower curtain than on the inside. As a result, the shower curtain blows inward.

A.J.C./J.T.

BERRY In botany, the word *berry* refers to a simple fruit having a skin or rind surrounding the seeds in a fleshy substance called pulp. Common kinds of berries are blueberries, grapes, tomatoes, citrus fruits, and melons. In spite of their names, strawberries, blackberries, and raspberries are not true berries. However, most people call any small, juicy fruit that has many seeds a berry. *See also* FRUIT.

P.G.C./F.W.S.

EXAMPLES OF BERRIES

holly berries

tomato

cucumber

lemon

melon

grapes

Berries have supplied food for people for many centuries. Animals in the wild also rely on a wide variety of berries for food.

BERYL (ber′əl) Beryl is a hard mineral found mainly in granite rocks and used as a gemstone. In the rocks in which it is found, beryl usually appears in the form of six-sided crystals, ranging in diameter from 0.25 in. [0.64 cm] to 12 in. [30 cm]. Some beryl crystals have been found in Maine measuring about 18 ft. [5 m] in length. Beryl is one of the most important sources of the rare element beryllium. Major deposits are located in Brazil, India, South Africa, and parts of the United States.

This is an example of yellow golden beryl.

Most often yellowish green in color, beryls may also be red, green, blue, or yellow. Types of beryl include the dark green emerald, the blue green aquamarine, the rose morganite, the yellow green hiddenite, and yellow golden beryl.

J.J.A./R.H.; E.W.L.

BERYLLIUM *See* BERYL; ELEMENT.

BERZELIUS, JÖNS JAKOB (1779-1848) Jöns Berzelius was a Swedish chemist who was the first person to make a fairly accurate list of the atomic weights. (*See* ATOMIC WEIGHT.) He also developed the chemical symbols and formulas in use today. He studied the effects of electricity on solutions, introducing the idea of radicals. (*See* RADICAL.)

Berzelius discovered the elements selenium, thorium, and silicon. Many of the terms used in chemistry, such as *catalyst, isomer,* and *protein,* were first used by Berzelius. Because of his many accomplishments, Jöns Berzelius was the most famous chemist of his time. *See also* CHEMISTRY, HISTORY OF. J.J.A./D.G.F.

BESSEMER, SIR HENRY (1813-1898) Sir Henry Bessemer was an English inventor who developed an inexpensive process for making steel. The Bessemer process, introduced in 1856, blasts air through molten pig iron (crude iron) to burn out the impurities. This method greatly reduced the cost of producing steel. It has since been modified by using pure oxygen instead of air. (*See* STEEL.)

Bessemer was a self-educated engineer. In addition to his work with steel, he developed a solar furnace, a large telescope, and a type of gold powder used to tint paint.

A.J.C./D.G.F.

BETA CENTAURI *See* STAR.

BETA PARTICLE (bāt′ə pärt′i kəl) Beta particles are electrons sent out in streams by the nuclei of certain radioactive atoms. Most beta particles are negatively charged, but some are positively charged and are called positrons. The streams of beta particles are often called beta rays. These rays travel at a speed almost equal to that of light. Having such high energy, beta rays can pass through solid matter several millimeters thick. They ionize the substances through which they pass. Beta particles can be detected by Geiger counters and by photographic film. The other kinds of radiation produced by radioactive substances are alpha particles and gamma rays. *See also* ALPHA PARTICLE; GAMMA RAY; GEIGER COUNTER; IONS AND IONIZATION; RADIO-ACTIVITY. J.J.A./J.T.

BETELGEUSE *See* STAR.

BICEPS (bī′seps′) The biceps are muscles found in the human body. One bicep is attached to the front side of the upper arm. Its action has the effect of bending the arm and helping in the rotation of the hand. It is called the biceps brachii. A person can feel the contraction of his or her biceps brachii when he or she turns a screwdriver. Another muscle, the biceps femoris, is found at the back of the upper leg. It allows the leg to bend at the knee and helps the lower leg rotate to the side when the knee is bent. The biceps femoris also helps the other leg muscles straighten the thigh at the hip joint. P.G.C./L.V.C.; J.J.F.

BIENNIAL PLANT Biennial (bī′en′ē əl) plants live for only two years. In the first year, they grow strong roots and leaves. Food is

An important biennial plant in many parts of the world is the beet plant. Biennial plants live for two years.

stored in the roots for use during the second year. As winter approaches, biennial plants enter a time of dormancy, during which very little growth takes place.

In the second year, biennial plants use the stored food to produce flowers and seeds. Some biennial plants are carrots, beets, and cabbage. These vegetables are eaten after the first season, before the plant can flower.

A.J.C./M.H.S.

BIG BANG THEORY

The big bang theory is an explanation for the formation of the universe as it exists today. The theory suggests that, at one time, all matter in the universe existed as a black hole, which exploded about 7 to 20 billion years ago. (*See* BLACK HOLE.) Scientists refer to this explosion as the "big bang." The radiation given off from the explosion is referred to as the primordial fireball. *Primordial* refers to the earliest form of an object or organism. Over about 1 million years, the fireball gradually changed into matter. This matter eventually formed the sun, stars, planets, and other heavenly bodies. The galaxies in the universe are still separating from the force of the explosion. *See also* COSMOLOGY; UNIVERSE.

P.W./L.W.

BIG DIPPER AND LITTLE DIPPER

The most familiar groups of stars in the northern hemisphere are the Big Dipper and the Little Dipper. The Big Dipper and the Little Dipper each have seven stars. Four stars make up the corners of the cup shapes. Three stars make up the handles.

Both of these groups of stars revolve around the North Star. The North Star is almost directly over the North Pole and forms the tip of the handle of the Little Dipper. (*See* NORTH STAR.)

The Big Dipper is part of the Ursa Major, or Great Bear, constellation. The Little Dipper is part of the Ursa Minor, or Little Bear, constellation. *See also* CONSTELLATION.

A.J.C./E.W.L.; C.R.

BILE

Bile is a greenish yellow digestive fluid made in the liver and stored in the gallbladder. Bile helps the body neutralize acid and absorb fat. During digestion, bile travels to the small intestine. Once there, it breaks down fatty foods. *See also* DIGESTION.

P.W./J.E.P.

BIMETALLIC STRIP

A bimetallic (bī'mə-tal'ik) strip is made by fastening together two strips of different metals. The metals are often brass and iron. When different metals are heated, they expand by different amounts. This happens when a bimetallic strip is heated, and this causes the strip to bend. When it is cooled, the strip returns to its original shape. Bimetallic strips are used in some thermostats for controlling heating systems. When the temperature rises, the strip starts to bend. Eventually it bends so much that it stops the supply of gas or electricity to the heater. When the temperature drops to a certain point, the strip bends back again, and the supply is reconnected. Bimetallic strips are also used in circuit breakers, which are switches that stop or start the flow of an electric current. *See also* CIRCUIT BREAKER; EXPANSION.

M.E./J.T.

BINARY NUMBERS

Binary (bī'nə rē) numbers make up a number system that has 2 as its base. Every number system has a base, or quantity used as the starting point for calculation. The base of a number system can be any number at all. Throughout history, different number systems have been used by different cultures. The ancient Babylonians based their system on 60, the Romans on 12. The decimal system, based on 10, is used throughout the world now. With the coming of computers, the binary system, based on the number 2, has come into widespread use.

The kinds of numerals used in a number system depend on the base of the system. Ten symbols (0, 1, 2, 3, 4, 5, 6, 7, 8, 9) must be used for the decimal system. In the binary system, only two symbols (0 and 1) are used.

It is because of this that binary numbers are more helpful for use in computers than decimal numbers. The numeral 1 can be coded by the computer as a single electrical pulse. The numeral 0 can be coded as the lack of an electrical pulse. The computer term *bit* is taken from the words *binary digit*. Each zero or one is called a bit. Computers of a simple design use eight bits to code letters, numbers, and symbols. An eight-bit series of zeroes and ones is called a *byte*. The following are examples of bytes and the characters they represent:

$$01000001 = A$$
$$01000010 = B$$
$$00110001 = 1$$
$$00110010 = 2$$

Newer and faster computers can read more than one byte at a time. A sixteen-bit computer reads two bytes at a time, while a thirty-two bit computer reads eight bytes at once. *See also* COMPUTER. J.J.A./S.P.A.; W.J.F.; R.J.S.

BINDWEED (bīn′dwēd′) Bindweed is the name of a group of perennial plants belonging to the morning glory family. (*See* MORNING GLORY; PERENNIAL PLANT.) Bindweeds are found throughout the United States and southern Canada, as well as in Europe and parts of

Bindweeds, with their colorful, funnel-shaped flowers, are members of the morning glory family. They grow wild in many areas.

Asia. They grow along roads, beaches, and fields. The hedge bindweed and field bindweed often grow among cultivated crops, causing extensive damage. Bindweeds have arrow- or heart-shaped leaves and funnel-shaped flowers.   A.J.C./M.H.S.

BINET, ALFRED (1857-1911) Alfred Binet was a French psychologist who developed the first intelligence test for children. The French government asked Binet to design a test that could identify children who seemed to be less intelligent than the average. The learning ability of these children is usually much less than that of other children the same age. The purpose of the tests was to allow educators to decide which children needed special schooling.

In 1905, working with Theodore Simon, Binet developed the Binet-Simon intelligence tests. These were the first scales for measuring intelligence, or discovering "mental age." They helped teachers find out the relative intelligence of their students. Later, the tests were used to find a child's intelligence quotient (IQ). The IQ is a number equal to the mental age, as determined by testing, divided by the chronological, or actual, age of the person tested, and then multiplied by 100. If a person's intelligence is average, then his or her mental age and his or her chronological age are the same. Thus, the person's mental age divided by his or her chronological age is 1. When that is multiplied by 100, the answer is 100. Therefore, the IQ of an average person is 100. Many people have questioned the accuracy and purpose of IQ measurement, but intelligence tests are still used. *See also* INTELLIGENCE.

J.J.A./D.G.F.

BINOCULARS (bə näk′yə lərz) Binoculars are a pair of small telescopes built into a casing, or frame. (*See* TELESCOPE.) The telescopes allow stereoscopic vision, which is the ability to judge depth by using both eyes at the same time. Binoculars make distant objects seem closer by means of magnification. (*See* MAGNIFICATION.)

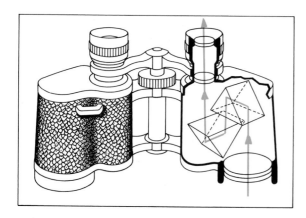

Binoculars are instruments designed for use with both eyes to achieve a close-up view of things from a distance. Each tube of the instrument contains two prisms. The arrows show how the light is bent four times as it passes through the instrument.

The two telescopes in binoculars are exactly alike. Each telescope is built into a funnel-shaped tube, or cylinder. An objective lens is at the wider end of each tube. An eyepiece, consisting of one or more lenses, is at the narrower end of each tube. Each tube contains two prisms located between the objective and eyepiece lenses. (*See* LENS; PRISM.)

The objective lenses gather light from the object being viewed. They form images that are upside down and reversed right-to-left. By bending the light beams, the prisms correct the image to proper orientation before it reaches the eyepiece lenses. The eyepiece lenses further magnify the image.

Most binoculars have adjusting wheels, or knobs, that change the distances between the objective lenses and the eyepiece lenses. This movement of the lenses closer or farther apart brings the object into focus. Some binoculars have one focus wheel for both telescope tubes. Higher-quality binoculars have controls for independent focus of each telescope.

Binoculars usually have two numbers printed or engraved somewhere on the outer covering. The first number is the power or magnification. The second number is the diameter of the objective lens in millimeters. Binoculars that are marked 6 × 35, for example, will magnify an object six times through an objective lens that is 1.4 in. [35 mm] in diameter.

Many modern microscopes are arranged in binocular fashion. This makes looking into the microscope more comfortable and gives the viewer a three-dimensional image.

G.M.B./S.S.B.

BIOCHEMISTRY (bī′ō kem′ə strē) Biochemistry is the science that studies the chemical makeup and processes of all living things. The whole structure of living things is built up from chemical substances. These substances are constantly changing. Complex molecules are being broken down into simpler parts. Simple parts are being built up again.

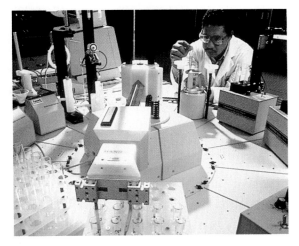

Biochemists have made important contributions to pharmacology (the study of drugs). Here, a scientist monitors a robot's testing of drugs for purity.

The study of biochemistry began in the late eighteenth century. Chemicals were taken from living things and studied. Since the late nineteenth century, biochemists have made many discoveries. Some important discoveries are connected with food and energy. Biochemists have discovered how plants use energy from the sun to build simple substances into more complex ones by photosynthesis. (*See* PHOTOSYNTHESIS.) They have found how animals break down foods by digestion into simpler parts, and then build these up again. Biochemists have also traced the complex series of reactions linked with the Krebs cycle. This cycle releases the energy in food molecules. (*See* KREBS CYCLE.) Biochemists have studied special molecules in the cell called nucleic acids. Scientists believe these acids may be the controllers of all growth and reproduction. One form of nucleic acid, RNA, is found throughout the cell,

where it controls the making of protein. DNA is another form of nucleic acid. DNA carries and passes a kind of "blueprint," or plan of a living thing, from one generation to the next. (*See* NUCLEIC ACID.) Biochemistry is also concerned with the workings of membranes and with the chemical changes that take place in muscles as they contract and in nerve cells as they conduct messages.

Through its discoveries of how the body functions in health and sickness, biochemistry has contributed to medicine. It has led to the understanding and treatment of diseases in which the body's chemistry goes wrong. Pharmacology, the study of drugs and their actions, is closely related to biochemistry. (*See* PHARMACOLOGY.) Techniques of biochemistry, such as chemical analysis, chromatography, and the use of radioisotopes as "tracers," are valuable in the study of many diseases. (*See* CHROMATOGRAPHY; TRACER.) Biochemists are helping learn some of the causes of mental illness, the origins of birth defects, and how poor diet affects intelligence.   J.J.A./E.R.L.

BIODEGRADABILITY (bī ō di grād′ə bil′-ətē) Biodegradability refers to the ability of a substance to decompose, or be broken down, by microorganisms. (*See* DECOMPOSITION; MICROORGANISM.) Examples of substances in nature that are biodegradable are leaves, bodies of animals, and oil. Many human-made products, such as Styrofoam and plastics, are not biodegradable. Many areas in the United States are running out of places to store these wastes. These substances will build up and pollute the environment. To help control this pollution, scientists are researching ways to make some human-made substances, such as plastics, biodegradable.   C.C./J.E.P.

BIOFEEDBACK (bī'ō fēd' bak') Biofeedback is a method of becoming aware of involuntary body processes, such as blood pressure and body temperature. Once aware of these processes, a person may learn to exercise some voluntary control over them.

The way a person becomes aware of these body processes is by being connected to different biofeedback machines by electrodes. An electrode is an electrical conductor by which an electric current enters or leaves an object. The machine measures body processes and conveys information about them to the person through a tone or display on a computer screen. For example, if a person's blood pressure falls below a certain level, a tone might sound. The person can learn to lower his or her blood pressure by first recalling how he or she felt when the tone sounded. The person then concentrates on achieving the feeling again.

Many biofeedback machines measure the electrical signals given off by muscle contractions. Muscles constractions can indicate tension. By learning to control tension, other problems may be cured. For example, bedwetting problems are linked to tense pelvic muscles. Children who can learn how to keep their pelvic muscles relaxed through biofeedback may be able to stop wetting their beds. Similarly, headaches may be the result of tense neck muscles. Headaches may be prevented by learning how to keep the neck muscles relaxed. Other biofeedback devices may detect tiny amounts of perspiration on the skin, which is also linked to tension. Biofeedback recordings of very slight muscle activity have helped some patients gain slight control over areas thought to be paralyzed. Biofeedback has also been found to help other conditions, such as stuttering and asthma. (*See* ASTHMA.)

Biofeedback is gaining wide acceptance. People who are interested in self improvement seek out biofeedback specialists. Physicians may also advise patients with certain difficulties to try biofeedback.   P.W./J.E.P.

BIOLOGICAL CONTROL (bī'ə läj'i kəl) Biological control is a method of fighting pests by using their natural enemies against them. Natural enemies are used instead of artificial means, such as chemical pesticides. (*See* PESTICIDE.) For example, cats naturally feed on mice, so cats are often used by humans to kill mice around the home. Biological control is used on a much larger scale on farms. Farmers bring natural enemies, such as certain disease-causing organisms, into their fields to reduce the amount of harmful pests. For example, the organism *myxomatosis* causes disease among rabbits. It has been used in Australia to reduce the number of rabbits, which once caused widespread crop damage. (*See* DISEASE.)

Plants are another method of biological control. For example, mint, garlic, and marigolds produce chemicals that repel certain insects. Gardeners often plant these flowers among their other flowers or vegetables to keep away plant-damaging insects. The release of sterile (infertile) male insects into an area where plants are being raised is another method of biological control. Many female insects mate only once. Thus, if they mate with one of the sterilized males, they will not be fertilized, and no young will be produced.

Scientists are researching new methods of biological control. For example, they are researching ways to produce a type of bacteria that would be added to the soil in which plants are being raised. This bacteria would kill certain disease-causing organisms among plants. Scientists are also researching a fungus

Biological control fights pests by means of their natural enemies. At left, insects that are harmless to people are put in a position to eat the eggs of another insect that is a serious pest to people.

that is fatal to gypsy moths. Gypsy moths cause harm to forests in the northeastern United States. Scientists are studying how to quicken the effects of the fungus on the gypsy moth and how to safely release the fungus into a given area. Scientists are also trying to change the genes of certain vegetables so they produce their own chemical insect repellents. (*See* GENETICS.)

No method of biological control has been found to be completely effective. Thus, chemical pesticides are still used. Unfortunately, chemical pesticides sometimes kill desirable pests as well as the pests they are meant to control. Scientists hope that improved methods of biological control will gain an increasing role in controlling pests. They believe that this may someday mean the end of the release of polluting chemicals into the environment. *See also* INSECT. P.Q.F./J.E.P

BIOLOGICAL RHYTHM (bī′ə läj′i kəl rith′əm) Cycles that occur regularly in living things are called biological rhythms. Sleeping is a biological rhythm in humans because humans sleep every day. Some rhythms involve behavior, such as sleeping. Other rhythms involve body functions, such as heartbeat.

Biological rhythms occur without the organism's completely controlling them. For example, a person's heart beats constantly, he or she sleeps regularly, and his or her blood pressure changes in response to various situations. The person can exercise some control over some of these rhythms—for example, by delaying sleep for a certain amount of time. However, the person cannot totally control the rhythms. For the most part, they happen by themselves.

No one knows exactly how biological rhythms work. Scientists believe that organisms have a "built-in clock" that "tells" the organisms what time of day it is. For instance, certain species of mice are only active at night. When these mice are kept in a cage that is dark all day, they still sleep during the day and are active at night. Their "built-in clock" apparently tells them when night has come, even though their eyes cannot tell.

There are several kinds of biological rhythms. Some happen twice a day. For example, crabs come out of their holes at every low tide. Some kinds of biological rhythms happen once a day, such as humans sleeping. These daily rhythms are called *diurnal* or *circadian*, both of which come from Latin words referring to day. (*See* DIURNAL RHYTHM.) Other rhythms happen once a month, such as the menstrual cycle in women. These cycles are called *lunar*, which refers to the moon. Annual rhythms happen once a year, such as flowers blossoming on a plant in the spring. S.R.G./E.R.L.

BIOLOGY (bī äl′ə jē) Biology is the science that studies all living things. Because the cell is considered to be the basic unit of life, all organisms that are made up of one or more cells are clearly in the domain of biology. (*See* CELL; CLASSIFICATION OF LIVING ORGANISMS; LIFE.)

There are some organisms, however, that are acellular, or not made up of cells. A virus, for example, has no characteristics of life when it is studied in the isolated state. (*See* VIRUS.) When present in a living cell, however, a virus can cause the reproduction of other viruses like itself. Because reproduction is a characteristic of living organisms, many scientists consider the virus to be alive.

History of biology People have been interested in biology since prehistoric times. They realized that some things were living or had been living while other things had never been alive. It was not until the time of the ancient Greek and Roman civilizations, however, that biological observations were written down and recorded for future generations. The Greek philosopher Aristotle is often considered to have been the first biologist. (*See*

ARISTOTLE.) With the fall of these cultures in the first few centuries A.D., interest in the sciences declined. For almost a thousand years, superstition and magic obscured scientific progress.

In the sixteenth century, Sir Francis Bacon played a large role in reawakening scientific curiosity. (*See* BACON, FRANCIS.) In the years that followed, many other scientists began studying living things. With the invention of the microscope in the seventeenth century, a whole new world was opened to the scientist— the previously unseen world of the cell. (*See* MICROSCOPE.) Biology, once a purely descriptive science, now became an experimental science. It was not enough for biologists to see something happen. They wanted to know how and why it was happening, and they devised experiments to discover the answers. By the nineteenth century, biology had been established as a major field of scientific research. In the following decades, the understanding of life and related biological knowledge increased at a rapid rate.

Fields of biology Biology is usually divided into two major fields: botany and zoology. (*See* BOTANY; ZOOLOGY.) Botany is the study of the plant kingdom, and zoology is the study of the animal kingdom. Since many organisms do not fit into either of these fields, some biologists consider a third major field to be microbiology, the study of all microscopic forms of life. (*See* MICROBIOLOGY.)

These major fields are subdivided into ten broad areas of study. Anatomy deals with the structure of living things. Biochemistry deals with chemicals and chemical reactions that affect life. Biological earth science uses the earth sciences in the study of living things. Biomathematics uses mathematics to study life. Biophysics studies the physical properties that affect life. Ecology studies the relationships between living organisms and between organisms and their environment. Pathology studies diseases that affect living organisms. Physiology studies the functions of living things. Biological psychology studies the psychology of living things. Taxonomy names and classifies living organisms. (*See* ANATOMY; BIOCHEMISTRY; BIOPHYSICS; ECOLOGY; PATHOLOGY; PHYSIOLOGY; PSYCHOLOGY; TAXONOMY.)

An entomologist (zoologist who studies insects) is artificially producing queen bees.

The discoveries biologists make and the techniques they develop have a direct effect on our lives. Someday, biologists may find the answers to problems of today's world such as overpopulation and pollution. They are also working more closely with scientists in other fields. Sciences such as physics and chemistry were once totally separate from biology. Modern biologists, however, must have a good knowledge of other sciences so that they can understand their own field. With this awareness, biologists can increase our knowledge of the basic workings of life. *See also* SCIENCE.

A.J.C./E.R.L.

BIOLUMINESCENCE (bī′ō lü′mə nes′ns) Bioluminescence is the production of light by living things. This biochemical reaction results in very little heat. Many bioluminescent creatures live so deep in the oceans that light from the sun never reaches them. These creatures use their bioluminescence to attract mates and, in some cases, to attract prey. They do not use this light to see where they are going.

The blinking of fireflies as they signal their mates on summer evenings is an example of bioluminescence. Some bacteria and fungi also show bioluminescence. *See also* FIREFLY; LUMINESCENCE.

A.J.C./E.R.L.

BIOMASS (bī′ō mas′) Biologists and other scientists use *biomass* to describe populations of living things in terms of their total weight or volume within a given area, or habitat. Biomass can be a measure of all the living things in a habitat, a given species in a habitat, or a group of species in a habitat. For example, the biomass of a rain forest could include the weight or volume of all the plants and animals that live in it. The biomass of a particular body of water could refer to one particular species, such as the shrimp, that lives there.

Biomass can also refer to renewable energy sources, such as trees. Examples of nonrenewable energy sources are coal and oil. Biomass materials, such as wood, sawdust, grain, and aquatic plants, can be used to produce energy. For example, the materials can

Scientists are experimenting with the use of aquatic plants, such as these being removed from a Florida canal, as a source of energy. Such renewable energy sources are called biomass.

be burned to produce heat. Also, certain processes can convert biomass into a synthetic, or human-made, form of oil. This oil is called biocrude. Many scientists believe biomass will be an increasingly important energy source as nonrenewable energy sources are depleted. *See also* AQUATIC PLANT; ENERGY.

P.Q.F./J.E.P.

BIOME (bī'ōm') A biome is a large natural area that has a particular climate, plants, animals, and other characteristics that make it different from other areas. Rain forests, tundras (cold, treeless plains), savannas (tropical grasslands), and deserts are examples of different land biomes. An ocean is an example of an aquatic biome. The plants and animals that live in a biome are adapted to its particular conditions, such as temperature, rainfall, and soil type. *See also* ECOLOGY; ECOSYSTEM.

P.Q.F./J.E.P.

BIOPHYSICS (bī'ō fiz'iks) Biophysics is a relatively recent scientific discipline that combines the special interests of physics and chemistry with those of biology. Most of the research in biophysics has been done by physicists with a strong interest in biology. The methods of physics and chemistry are used to study and to explain the structures of living organisms, the mechanics of life processes, and the cooperative biological interactions that are essential to life.

The biophysicist describes biological processes in physical terms. His or her research is subject to laboratory experiments and testing, mathematical measurements, biochemical analysis, and other means of precise physical interpretation.

The recent growth of biophysics is largely the result of the development of biophysical tools and instruments that measure, describe, and analyze biological processes and functions.

Some of these instruments include electron microscopes, X-ray equipment, radioisotope scanners, ultracentrifuges, oscilloscopes, spectroscopes, electronic amplifiers, computers, and electronic monitoring devices. The term *medical physics* is often used to refer to work done using radiological instruments. (*See* RADIOLOGY.)

In the nineteenth century, physicists and anatomists conducted many experiments on living tissues. Using a galvanometer, the scientists discovered that minute electrical currents were generated in muscles and across nerve membranes. (*See* GALVANOMETER.) Further research led to the study of neurophysiology and the electrical nature of nerve impulses. Such investigations provided early research for the field of biophysics.

From 1895 to 1900, experiments by Henri Becquerel, Pierre and Marie Curie, and Ernest Rutherford (with radioactivity) and Wilhelm Roentgen (with X rays) provided unique tools for the growth of biophysics. (*See* BECQUEREL, ANTOINE HENRI; CURIE FAMILY; ROENTGEN, WILHELM CONRAD; RUTHERFORD, ERNEST.) In the 1920s, George de Heresy discovered that radioactive tracers follow the course of bodily substances. (*See* RADIOACTIVITY; TRACER; X RAYS.)

Electronic and atomic instruments developed during World War II (1939-1945) were significant for biophysics. Radar and sonar devices, which were used to detect aircraft, ships, and submarines, gave rise to the development of improved electronic equipment. The atomic bomb was developed with the aid of nuclear reactors. Following the war, these reactors provided an abundant supply of radioactive isotopes, which have been of great value in biophysical research and related fields. (*See* NUCLEAR ENERGY.)

With the development of the electron microscope, cells and tissues could be scanned and magnified more than 400,000 times. (*See* ELECTRON MICROSCOPE.) This made it possible to observe the physical activity of molecules and enzymes (proteins that cause or speed up chemical reactions) and to describe the structural activity of muscular contraction.

Biophysicists also study and explain the interchange of gases between the lungs and the blood and between the blood and the cells. They examine the effects of light, heat, cold, noise, pressure, and other forces on the physiology of living things. They study sensory communication and the mechanics of seeing, hearing, tasting, smelling, and feeling. They examine the complex relationship between stimulus and action.

Some of the most important applications of biophysics relate to surgical procedures, hospital patient care, nuclear medicine, and medical engineering. Biophysical instruments are used to diagnose and treat cancers and viral, circulatory, and kidney diseases. Diagnostic radiological instruments are used to image various body areas in order to locate tumors. Radiation therapy machines can give exact doses of radiation to control certain tumors. (*See* NUCLEAR MEDICINE; RADIATION THERAPY.) In research laboratories, biophysicists examine the physical activities that cause the death of cells, tissues, and whole organisms, and try to discover the causes of cell mutations (changes) and uncontrolled cancerous growths.

Patient monitoring systems and intensive care units use biophysical instruments before, during, and after surgery. Pulse, body temperature, and blood pressure are monitored. The electrical activity of the brain, heart, and other vital organs is tracked on monitoring devices.

Biophysicists and biomedical engineers have developed electronic aids for the deaf and the blind, artificial arms and legs, and orthopedic implants to replace worn hip and knee joints. Kidney dialysis machines enable people with damaged kidneys to go on living relatively normal lives. Bionics, a recent branch of biophysics, uses electronic devices to do the work of impaired organs. The electronic pacemaker is an example of one of these devices. The potential for biophysical research instruments valuable to the diagnosis and treatment of diseases is virtually unlimited. *See also* BIOCHEMISTRY; BIOLOGY; CHEMISTRY; MOLECULAR BIOLOGY; PHYSICS; PHYSIOLOGY.   D.A.T./G.D.B.; A.C.R.

BIOSPHERE (bī′ə sfir′) *Biosphere* is a term used to describe the parts of the earth and the thin layer of air above its surface that support life. The biosphere includes soil, the waters of the earth, and the lower atmosphere. *See also* ATMOSPHERE; EARTH.

W.R.P./R.J.B.

BIRCH The birches are a family of about forty trees and shrubs that grow in the cold and moderate-climate areas of North America, Europe, and Asia. Most birches have thin, easily peeled bark and tall, slender trunks growing in pairs or larger groups. Flowers are produced either on a male catkin in the fall, or on a female catkin in the spring. (*See* CATKIN.)

Birches grow well in poor soil and are often used for ornamental purposes. The sap produces an oil that can be used to make birch beer.

There are several common species of birches in the United States. The yellow birch (*Betula lutea*) is one of the most common. It grows to 50 to 82.5 ft. [15 to 25 m] high. It

may be silver, yellow, or gray when mature. The bark is loose and peels off naturally. Its hard wood is good for furniture. The paper birch (*Betula papyrifera*) grows to 60 to 82.5 ft. [18 to 25 m] high. It has thin, white bark. The bark was used by American Indians to build birchbark canoes. *See also* ALDER.

A.J.C./M.H.S.

BIRD Birds are warm-blooded animals of the class Aves. Like mammals, they are vertebrates. They are different from most mammals in that they do not bear live young but lay eggs from which the young are hatched. Birds have feathers, wings, and beaks that make them different from all other animals and easy to identify. (*See* EGG; FEATHER; MAMMAL; VERTEBRATE.)

Birds evolved from reptiles during the age of dinosaurs. Evolution of feathers from reptilian scales helped make flight possible. (*See* ARCHAEOPTERYX.) The adaptation to flight is probably responsible for the large number and wide distribution of birds. There are more birds than all other terrestrial (land-dwelling) vertebrates combined.

Most birds are good fliers, but there are a few so-called flightless kinds, such as the ostriches and the penguins. The penguins' wings have changed into swimming flippers in the millions of years since they first appeared on earth. The ostriches move about on their long, strong legs. Their wings are too small and weak to enable them to fly.

Birds use aerodynamic principles of lift and thrust in flying. (*See* AERODYNAMICS.) Their light, feathered wings and hollow bones help keep them as light as possible. By flapping their wings, they are able to produce thrust. Some birds, once they are aloft, glide and soar on air currents with almost no effort.

Penguins (top left) are flightless birds that live in Antarctica. Swans (top right) are large water birds with long, arched necks. They live in many parts of the world. Ostriches (shown with newborns at bottom) are large, flightless birds that live in Africa and parts of southwest Asia.

Pelicans are large water birds that live in warm areas. Despite their size and awkward appearance, they are graceful in the air. Many catch the fish on which they live by diving into the water from the air.

Vultures and albatrosses are birds that can soar for hours, barely flapping their wings.

There are about nine thousand species of birds. They range in size from the tiny hummingbird, about 2 in. [5 cm] in length, to the ostrich, which can grow to 8 ft. [2.5 m] in height and can weigh as much as 300 lb. [136 kg].

Birds live in most regions of the world, from the arctic to the tropics. They have adapted their behavior to the different climates and geographic regions.

The royal crane is a large African wading bird. It is sometimes kept as a pet.

Birds have no teeth. Instead, they have light, horny beaks with which they gather food, and a toughened part of the alimentary canal, called the gizzard, in which the food is chewed. (*See* ALIMENTARY CANAL.) This means that food is chewed near the bird's center of gravity, which helps it in flying.

Birds eat mainly insects, seeds, and animal flesh. Their beaks vary in shape and size depending on what they eat. The insect-eating birds, such as the starlings, have thin beaks

Owls are birds of prey. They usually hunt at night and are aided greatly by their keen vision and hearing and their ability to fly almost noiselessly.

with which they can probe into cracks and crevices. Birds that eat seeds, such as sparrows, have strong beaks to crack the shells of the seeds. Flesh-eating birds, such as the hawk and the owl, have beaks that are hooked. They can tear at the skin and meat of their prey.

Each species of bird has its own form of courtship behavior before nesting. For example, the grebes do a courtship dance on the ponds and lakes where they nest. Other birds have elaborate ways of flitting about, bobbing their heads, and strutting during courtship.

Birds sing to attract mates and to warn other birds away from their nesting area. In all species of songbirds, the male is usually the singer. Not all bird songs are beautiful. For example, the mockingbird has its own harsh call, but can imitate the songs of other birds.

The crow has a very unmusical "caw." Birds have various calls other than songs, such as alarm signals, calls of aggressiveness, calls to parents, and calls begging for food.

Two members of the parrot family are shown at left: the masked lovebird (top) and the great black cockatoo (bottom).

After courtship, most birds make nests in which to lay their eggs. The nests may be simple hollowed-out places in the ground, or they may be complicated, woven from grass and other soft materials. In some species, the male constructs the nest. In others, the female does so. Both sexes cooperate in certain species.

The newly laid eggs in the nest must be kept warm until they hatch. This is usually done by the birds sitting on the eggs. When the young birds hatch, they vary in their ability to move around. Ground-nesting and water-nesting species are feathered and alert when they are hatched and can look after themselves as soon as they leave the eggs. Most nestlings, however, are helpless in the nest and must be fed by their parents until they grow feathers and are able to fly. When they first fly from the nest, they are called fledglings.

Many birds migrate during certain seasons. (*See* MIGRATION.) They may fly long distances over land and water to warmer climates during winter. They return the next spring, usually to the same area, to mate and raise their young. The arctic terns are unusual in that they may travel 11,000 mi. [17,700 km] each way during their migrations from

Many birds, such as these blackbirds, migrate to warmer climates in winter. They return to their original homes in the spring.

their breeding grounds in the arctic to their wintering grounds in the antarctic. No one knows exactly how birds like these are able to navigate long distances over land and water. The subject has been studied by scientists for many years. It is possible that they use several methods, including knowing the direction in which the sun sets and knowing the positions of certain stars.

Birds are usually helpful to humans. They may eat harmful insects or rodents. Some birds can be destructive, though, such as those that eat seeds of farmers' crops.   P.G.C./L.S.

BISMUTH (biz′məth) Bismuth (Bi) is a brittle metallic element that is white with a reddish tint. Bismuth is sometimes found in nature as a free metal—that is, uncombined with other substances. It also occurs in minerals such as bismuth glance and bismite. (*See* ELEMENT; MINERAL.)

Bismuth is used mainly in making alloys that melt at low temperatures. (*See* ALLOY.) These alloys are used to make safety plugs in automatic sprinkler systems that put out fires. Heat melts the plugs, turning on the system when needed. Bismuth is also used for cooling in nuclear reactors. It is used for this because it does not easily absorb neutrons. Bismuth compounds are used in medicines and in making cosmetics. (*See* COMPOUND.)

Bismuth's atomic number is 83. Its atomic weight is 208.98. The melting point of bismuth is 520°F. [271°C], and its boiling point is 2,840°F. [1,560°C]. Its relative density is 9.7. *See also* RELATIVE DENSITY.　　M.E./J.R.W.

The American bison, commonly but incorrectly called the buffalo, once roamed the plains of North America in vast herds.

BISON (bīs′ən) *Bison* is the scientifically correct name for the North American wild animal often—but wrongly—called the buffalo. The bison (*Bison bison*) is a large member of the cattle family with shaggy brown hair and a large hump at the shoulder. The male may be 12.5 ft. [3.8 m] long and 6 ft. [1.8 m] tall, weighing as much as 3,080 lb. [1,400 kg] when fully grown. The female is much smaller, rarely weighing more than 900 lb. [408 kg].

Bison live and travel in herds. Although not fully mature until they are eight years old, bison start mating in their third year. A single calf is born in May or June. Although bison may live as long as forty years, most die before they are twenty-five years old.

In 1850, there were more than 20 million wild bison in the United States. By 1889, hunters had reduced this number to about 500. Strict laws were passed to stop this killing. The number of bison has since increased to about 40,000 in North America.

The beefalo is an animal produced by mating bison and cattle. Its meat is similar to beef but is less expensive. The beefalo, like the bison, does not need special grains for feed but instead grazes on grass and small plants.

A European bison called the wisent has become almost extinct due to uncontrolled hunting. The 1,500 remaining wisents are in zoos and game preserves.

　　　　　　　　　　　　　　　　A.J.C./J.J.M.

BIVALVE (bī′valv′)) A bivalve is an invertebrate animal that lives in water and belongs to the class Pelecypoda of the phylum Mollusca. (*See* INVERTEBRATE; MOLLUSCA.) *Bivalve* means "two valves," and the animal has a hard shell with two similar sides (valves) attached by a hinge at the back. This hinge allows the shell to open like a book. Types of bivalves include the clam, oyster, mussel, and scallop. Inside the shell is the soft, fleshy animal, which has a muscular foot but no head or legs. The animal feeds by extending a siphon, which acts as a straw to suck water into the shell and past the bivalve's mouth. Small organisms are filtered out of the water and eaten. The bivalve breathes by using its gills, which remove oxygen from the water sucked up by the siphon.

Scallops are typical bivalves that are an important source of food for humans.

Bivalves are found in both fresh and salt water. Most live on the bottom of an ocean, lake, or river, but others attach themselves with tough, sticky threads to rocks at the edge of the water. Many bivalves are popular as a food.   S.R.G./C.S.H.

Bivalve shellfish are mollusks in which the shell consists of two parts, or valves, that are hinged together. At the top are three views of a cockle, a typical bivalve. At the bottom is a scallop. Note the eyes around the rim.

BLACK BEAR The American black bear (*Ursus americanus*) lives in large forests throughout North America. Its coat is usually black, but other colors are not uncommon. The blue bear, actually black and gray, is a kind of black bear considered sacred by the Indians of southeast Alaska. The black bear grows to 5 ft. [1.5 m] in height and weighs between 200 and 500 lb. [91 and 227 kg]. The female usually gives birth to twins every other year.

There are about 75,000 black bears living in national forests in the United States. Black bears are good runners and may reach speeds of 25 m.p.h. [40 kph]. They are also good climbers and may rest in trees for hours at a time. Many bears living in national parks have lost their fear of human beings and may seem playful when begging for food. At times, though, these bears have attacked and killed the people who were feeding them.

Another variety of black bear is the Asiatic black bear (*Selenarctos thibetanus*). It is smaller than its American cousin, usually weighing less than 255 lb. [116 kg]. Also called the Himalayan black bear, it is found in the mountains and forests of south and east Asia. It has a V-shaped white marking on its chest and tufts of white hair on its chin. Many Chinese believe that the bones and meat of the Asiatic black bear have special healing powers. *See also* BEAR.   A.J.C./J.J.M.

BLACKBIRD The blackbird is a member of the American blackbird family, Icteridae, that includes red-winged blackbirds, bobolinks, grackles, meadowlarks, and orioles. The common European blackbird is actually a thrush,

Pictured is one of the many varieties of blackbirds: the yellow-headed blackbird, which makes its home in the marshes of North America.

very much like the American robin. The red-winged blackbird found throughout North America is about 8 in. [20 cm] long. Males are black with a red wing patch, and females are streaky brown. The bird nests in marshes and bushes near water. The bird uses its long, pointed bill to grasp insects from plants or from the ground. Blackbirds also eat seeds. *See also* BIRD.

W.R.P./L.L.S.

BLACK HOLE A black hole is an extremely dense collapsed star whose gravity is so strong that nothing, not even light, can escape from it. Usually, a black hole is a very large star nearing the end of its life. Black holes cannot be seen, but their existence can be inferred by observations. (*See* GRAVITY; STAR.)

In theory, when a star dies, it runs out of nuclear fuel. This causes the core of the star to cool and shrink. The tremendous mass of a large star then causes the star to collapse inwardly on itself until not even light can escape.

If the mass of the core of a collapsing star is less than 2.5 times that of our sun, the collapsing will stop before a black hole can form. If the mass of the star is greater than 0.08 times but less than 1.2 times that of our sun, astronomers call the star that is left a white dwarf. A white dwarf is very dense but can still radiate heat and light. If our sun were to collapse billions of years from now, it would become a white dwarf. If the mass of the collapsing star is between 1.2 and 2.5 times that of our sun, astronomers call the resulting star a neutron star.

If, however, the mass of the core exceeds that of the sun's by 2.5 times or more, the collapse will continue until a black hole forms. The size of the hole that forms will depend on the mass of the star. Gravitational collapse will compress (squeeze) a star so much that a body whose diameter was originally measured in millions of miles will form

This is the Milky Way galaxy, shown looking toward the center. Although the existence of black holes has not been proved, some astronomers think that as much as one-third of the Milky Way could be made up of black holes.

a black hole only a few miles in size. Because the density that results from such compression is so great and the gravitational force so strong, even the hole's own energy cannot escape from its surface. Astronomers can only visualize it as a completely dark, powerful, invisible mass.

The existence of black holes is still being studied by astronomers. Investigation of the possibility of black holes dates from 1917, when a German astronomer, Karl Schwarzschild, predicted that their existence would one day be verified. The theory of black holes was proposed to explain the irregular behavior of certain stars, which seemed to be under the influence of some invisible body.

Recent studies of X rays from outer space, using instruments mounted on space satellites, detected what seemed to be pairs of stars in orbit around each other. However, only one star was visible. The existence of the other, invisible, star (a black hole) could explain the variations in the X rays and the behavior of the visible star.

Present knowledge on black holes is increasing. Many theories have been offered to account for them and for their influence on other heavenly bodies. The strongest evidence for the existence of black holes is that X rays and other radiation have been detected coming from places in space where nothing can be seen but where something should be. Recently, some scientists have proposed the existence of singularities. A singularity is a black hole with a diameter of zero.

The next step toward verifying the existence of black holes is to find a way to improve visual observation of stars. The Hubble Space Telescope that was launched in 1990 may help astronomers decide whether black holes are what theory says they are. *See also* SOLAR SYSTEM.   P.G.Z./G.D.B.; D.H.M.

BLACK LIGHT Black light is ultraviolet, or invisible, light. It cannot be seen by the human eye because its rays lie beyond the violet end of the spectrum. However, black light can be "seen" in different ways. For instance, black light shows up on photographic film. It also causes certain oils, minerals, and chemicals to give off light. Black light is sometimes used to create special effects, such as dancing skeletons, on the stage. The skeletons are painted on black costumes with fluorescent paint. (*See* FLUORESCENCE.) Under black lights, only the paint shows. The rest of the costume cannot be seen. *See also* ULTRAVIOLET LIGHT.

G.M.B./S.S.B.

BLACKWELL, ELIZABETH (1821-1910) Elizabeth Blackwell was the first woman medical doctor in the United States. Blackwell is best known for her efforts to help women be accepted into medical colleges in the United States and Europe.

Blackwell was born in Bristol, England. She moved to the United States with her family when she was a child. Blackwell became a teacher in 1842 and studied medicine in her spare time. She applied to many medical colleges, but her application was rejected because she was a woman. Finally, in 1847, Blackwell was accepted by the Geneva Medical College in New York.

After she completed her medical degree, Blackwell applied for several positions in New York City. However, again, she was not hired because she was a woman. Blackwell then set up her own medical practice with her sister, Emily Blackwell. Emily had become a medical doctor shortly after Elizabeth. The

practice later became the New York Infirmary for Women and Children. Later, Blackwell organized a college as part of the infirmary. The college was run entirely by and for women.

During the Civil War (1861-1865), Blackwell led a group of nurses who helped wounded soldiers. In 1869, Blackwell opened another medical practice in London and helped found the London School of Medicine for Women. She taught gynecology at the school. Gynecology is a branch of medicine that deals with the health of women.   C.C./J.E.P.

BLACK WIDOW The black widow (wid′ō) spider is a poisonous species belonging to the family Theridiidae. It bears the name *widow* because the female often eats the male after mating. The female is shiny and black, and its body is about 0.5 in. [12.5 mm] long. It l as a

The black widow spider, found in many of the warmer parts of the world, has a dangerous bite. Usually, people do not die from its bite, but they suffer pain and paralysis.

red or yellowish pattern in the shape of an hourglass on the underside of the abdomen. The male is much smaller, reaching only 0.14 in. [4 mm] in length.

Black widow spiders usually live in warm regions. They often live in buildings. They eat insects that have become trapped in their webs. The black widow's bite does not usually kill a person, but a person may become sick for several days after being bitten. The poison of the North American black widow is stronger than that of the European variety. S.R.G./J.R.

BLAST FURNACE A blast furnace (fər′nəs) is a large (often several stories high), usually cone-shaped structure, made of a heat-resistant material such as brick or steel. Blast furnaces are used to make much of the world's iron supply through a process called smelting.

In smelting, iron is made by first "charging," or loading iron ore, coke (coal that has been heated to a high temperature without air), and crushed limestone into the top of a blast furnace through a large hole. A stream of very hot air is then blown into the furnace from the bottom. The hot air causes the coke to burn at very high temperatures. The air also combines with the carbon in the coke. The gas carbon monoxide is produced. This leaves the iron ore free of oxygen.

The burning coke produces the 3,000°F. [1,600°C] or higher temperatures needed to melt the iron out of the ore. Every four or five hours, workers remove a clay plug from a hole at the bottom of the furnace. This lets the melted iron flow out of the furnace. At the same time, the limestone, which has combined with impurities in the iron, flows out of the furnace on top of the iron. This limestone waste is called slag. It is disposed of. The iron is cast into large ingots, or slabs.

The iron made by blast furnaces is called crude or pig iron. Most of it is used later to make steel. Steel is made by melting the iron again and then blowing oxygen through it. Some iron, however, is remelted and cast into ornamental ironware and other items. It is then known as cast iron.

Blast furnaces are expensive and time consuming to build and operate. Also, they produce a great deal of pollution. This is also true of the ovens used to make the coke that the furnaces use as fuel. These problems have caused many iron producers to turn to other, cheaper and less polluting, methods of iron making. *See also* COKE; FURNACE; IRON; SMELTING; STEEL. P.Q.F./L.W.

BLIGHT (blīt′) A blight is a sudden, serious plant disease caused by a bacteria, fungus, or virus. (*See* BACTERIA; FUNGUS; VIRUS.) Blights are characterized by a rapid withering of parts of the diseased plants. Blights often reduce yields of crops such as corn, soybeans, and wheat. Blights also attack flowering plants, such as the rose.

The most damaging type of blight is caused by fungi. However, blights caused by fungi can be controlled by fungicides, chemicals that kill fungi. (*See* FUNGICIDE.) The second most damaging kind of blight is produced by a virus. The virus is passed from plant to plant by insects. Although the virus cannot easily be killed, the blight can be controlled by insecticides, chemicals that kill insects. (*See* INSECTICIDE.) A less harmful type of blight is caused by bacteria. However, blight caused by bacteria is difficult to control. P.Q.F./J.E.P.

BLOOD (bləd) Blood is the fluid that supplies the cells of the human body with the food and oxygen they need for work and growth. On its way from the heart, blood also carries heat to all parts of the body. On its way back to the heart, it helps remove carbon dioxide and other waste products. It contains special cells that help fight infection. It also forms solid clots to temporarily close wounds in the skin.

Red blood cells, magnified ten thousand times, are pictured at left. The scientific name for these cells is erythrocytes. The red coloring of erythrocytes comes from their oxygen-carrying hemoglobin.

Human blood is red because it contains hemoglobin, which is a red pigment. (*See* HEMOGLOBIN.)

The amount of blood in a human body depends upon the size of the person. The total volume of blood is about 8 percent of body weight. A 160 lb. [73 kg] man has about 6 qt. [5.6 liters] of blood. An 80 lb. [36 kg] child has about 2.5 qt. [2.8 liters]. A 9 lb. [4 kg] infant has about 5.4 oz. [0.3 liters]. People who live in high altitudes have 2 qt. [1.9 liters] about more blood than people who live in low regions. The extra blood carries the extra oxygen needed by the body at high altitudes.

Human blood, called whole blood, consists of solid particles floating in a straw-colored liquid called plasma. Plasma is made up of water, proteins, sugars, salts, and other substances. (*See* PLASMA.) The particles consist of red and white blood cells, or corpuscles, and smaller particles, called platelets. The plasma contains many proteins, including albumin, globulin, and fibrinogen. Albumin helps the blood retain water by drawing it from body tissue by osmosis. (*See* OSMOSIS.) Globulin contains antibodies that fight dis-

ease. (*See* ANTIBODY.) Fibrinogen combines with chemicals released by platelets to form blood clots.

Red blood cells, or erythrocytes, are formed in the bone marrow. (*See* MARROW.) They are tiny disks, about 0.00028 in. [0.007 mm] in diameter, and resemble doughnuts when seen through a microscope. The human body is constantly forming red blood cells. Red blood cells live for 120 days. Old red cells are destroyed in the bone marrow, spleen, and elsewhere at the rate of 2 million cells per second. (*See* SPLEEN.)

White blood cells, or leucocytes, are mostly formed in the bone marrow. White cells are larger than red cells. They average 0.00028 to 0.00048 in. [0.007 to 0.012 mm] in diameter. White cells have a nucleus, or center, unlike red cells. White cells protect the body against fight infection. Neutrophils are white cells that fight bacterial infection. They are the most numerous type of white cells. Lymphocytes are white cells that control immunity, a process that helps protect the body against infection by bacteria, viruses, and other foreign substances. A third type of white blood cell, called a monocyte, consumes bacteria and works with lymphocytes during immune reactions. (*See* IMMUNITY.)

Sometimes, a particularly massive infection may spread from the injured part of the body into the blood itself. This condition is referred to as sepsis, or blood poisoning. Sepsis includes such symptoms as fever, shock, skin rash, and hypothermia. Hypothermia is a condition in which body temperature drops dangerously low. Sepsis is treated with large doses of antibiotics. (*See* ANTIBIOTIC.)

Platelets are tiny disks 0.00008 to 0.00016 in. [0.002 to 0.004 mm] in diameter. They help prevent loss of blood. If a small blood vessel is cut or broken, platelets stick to the damaged edges and to each other. As they pile up, they form a temporary seal over the injury. At the same time, platelets release a substance that starts the process of blood clotting. Blood clots are larger "plugs" that prevent additional loss of blood.

People with too few platelets in their blood bleed a great deal before their blood clots. A small cut could cause a person to bleed to death if blood did not clot. Some people have blood that does not clot properly. This is a serious condition called hemophilia. (*See* HEMOPHILIA.)

Blood pressure is the pressure that blood exerts on the walls of the arteries. (*See* ARTERY.) The amount of pressure depends upon the strength of the heart muscle, the amount of blood in the circulatory system, and the condition of the arteries. Measurements of blood pressure are given with two numbers, such as *120/80*. This is expressed verbally as 120 over 80. The first number represents the pressure when the heart is contracting. It is called the systolic pressure. The second number represents the pressure when

the heart is relaxing. It is called the diastolic pressure. Normal pressure for adults is 120/80. (*See* HEART.)

Systolic blood pressure usually rises with age because the arteries become less flexible. As the arteries become less flexible, the same volume of blood passes through them, but pressure is higher because the arteries do not expand as much with each heartbeat. High blood pressure, also called hypertension, can contribute to heart disease, kidney disease, or stroke. (*See* STROKE.) Excessive weight and lack of exercise can contribute to hypertension. Low blood pressure is called hypotension. It rarely indicates serious disease, unless a person is bleeding a great deal.

Most animals, including fish, birds, and insects, have blood in their bodies. The blood is usually red. However, some invertebrates (animals without a backbone) have blood that contains a protein called hemocyanin. It causes their blood to be blue in color. Insect blood can be green, yellow, or colorless. *See also* BLOOD TYPES; CIRCULATORY SYSTEM; HEMOCYANIN.   P.Q.F.; W.R.P./L.V.C.; J.J.F.; M.H.M.

BLOODSUCKER *See* LEECH.

BLOOD TRANSFUSION Blood transfusion (blɔd trans fyü′zhən) is the process of putting whole blood or blood plasma into a person's body to replace blood lost through sickness or injury. (*See* BLOOD.) This process has saved millions of lives. It is especially helpful in counteracting shock, a common cause of death in accident victims.

The discovery of blood types by the Austrian-American scientist, Karl Landsteiner, in 1900 made blood transfusions practical on a large scale. (*See* BLOOD TYPES.) At first, donors came to the patient's bedside, and blood was transferred directly. Then, in 1914, it was discovered that blood could be stored for a short period of time. It had to be refrigerated, and a chemical that prevented clotting had to be added. Today, blood and blood components for transfusion are collected from donors and stored in blood banks.

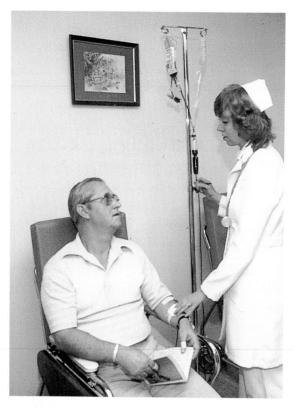

A blood transfusion is given to replace blood lost through accident or illness. Supplies of blood are stored in blood banks.

Most blood banks are operated by the American Red Cross. The blood is stored in plastic bags and classified by type. Whole blood can be stored for three weeks. Certain components of blood that have been separated from whole blood can be frozen and stored for several years. Blood banks in the United States collect more than 9 million pints of blood a year. Blood donors are normal, healthy volunteers who are screened

carefully by the blood bank to make sure that they do not have any disease, such as AIDS, that may be transmitted by their blood. (*See* AIDS.) They donate about a pint of blood each session and rarely notice any side effects. Although the bone marrow quickly replenishes the amount of blood that has been donated, blood donors are not allowed to give blood more often than every two months.

Before a transfusion is given, the patient's blood is tested to determine its ABO and Rh groups. Donor blood with the same types is selected. Another test, called a cross match, makes sure that the blood of both patient and donor can be mixed together without causing a harmful reaction. The plastic bag containing the blood is hung on a stand above the patient's bed. The blood flows down through a plastic tube, through a hollow needle that has been inserted in the patient's arm, and into a vein. The rate of flow is carefully controlled.

W.R.P./L.V.C.; J.J.F.

BLOOD TYPES Human blood (blǝd) is classified into blood types based on the presence or absence of certain antigens on red blood cells. (*See* BLOOD.) Antigens are special proteins. If certain antibodies (another kind of protein) are mixed with blood, they react with these antigens and cause the red blood cells to clump together. (*See* ANTIBODY.) Clumping can block small blood vessels and result in serious illness or death. Blood types, or blood groups, are important in blood transfusions. When one person's blood is being given to another, the recipient's blood plasma could contain antibodies that react with the antigens on the donor's red blood cells, causing clumping. (*See* BLOOD TRANSFUSION.)

Blood types are inherited. There are two major grouping systems, the ABO system and the Rh system. The ABO system was developed in 1900 by the Austrian-American scientist Karl Landsteiner. He determined that blood can be one of four types: A, B, AB, or O. As the chart shows, type A contains only the antigen called A. Type B contains only the antigen called B. Types A and B contain antibodies in the plasma against the antigens that are not present on the red blood cells. Type AB contains both A and B antigens. Type AB contains no antibodies in the plasma. Type O contains no antigens, but it does contain both anti-A and anti-B antibodies.

CLASSIFYING BLOOD INTO TYPES		
BLOOD TYPE	ANTIGENS ON RED BLOOD CELLS	ANTIBODIES IN PLASMA
A	A	B
B	B	A
AB	A & B	NONE
O	NONE	A & B

Doctors prefer to use identical ABO blood types during transfusions to avoid any possibility of clumping. In emergencies, type O blood can be given to anyone—it is the universal donor. Type AB can receive blood from anyone in an emergency when the specific type is not available. Type AB is called the universal recipient. About 45 percent of Americans have type O blood, 41 percent have type A, 10 percent have type B, and 4 percent have type AB. Recent studies have shown that there may be a relationship between blood types and certain diseases. For instance, people with type A blood are more likely to get cancer of the stomach than are people with other blood types.

In 1940, Landsteiner and Alexander S. Wiener, an American scientist, discovered an additional important factor, the rhesus, or Rh, factor. About 85 percent of Americans have the Rh factor on the surface of their red blood cells. Their blood is called Rh-positive. People who lack this factor have Rh-negative blood. Those with Rh-negative blood may produce anti-Rh antibodies in their plasma.

An Rh-positive patient can receive a transfusion from an Rh-negative donor. If an Rh-negative patient receives Rh-positive blood, however, antibodies will be produced. These antibodies will not usually have an effect unless a second Rh-positive transfusion is given. Then, the anti-Rh antibodies will attack the antigens on the Rh-positive blood cells and cause clumping.

A similar situation may occur if an Rh-negative mother and an Rh-positive father have a child. Since blood types are inherited, the child may be Rh-positive. Before being born, the baby's blood may cause production of anti-Rh antibodies by the mother. This will not have an effect on the first child. If the mother becomes pregnant with another Rh-positive baby, her antibodies may react with the baby's red blood cell Rh antigens. This can result in clumping and in destruction of the red blood cells in the baby, causing anemia or brain damage. (*See* ANEMIA.) If the second child (or any others) is born suffering from this disease, which is called hemolytic disease of the newborn, the baby's blood can be replaced with fresh blood. This will prevent most serious damage. In recent years, physicians have developed a serum to prevent an Rh-negative mother from producing anti-Rh antibodies during her pregnancy. *See also* SERUM.

A.J.C./L.V.C; M.J.C.; J.J.F.

BLUEBIRD The bluebird is a small bird that is a kind of thrush. (*See* THRUSH.) It is related to the robin. There are three species of bluebirds. The eastern bluebird is found in central and eastern North America. The western bluebird and mountain bluebird are found west of the Rocky Mountains in the United States and Canada and in western Mexico.

Bluebirds gather in small flocks when not nesting. They grow to be 6 in. [15 cm] long. The male eastern bluebird has a dark blue back. The male western bluebird has a rusty back. Both have blue wings, orange breasts, and white bellies. The male mountain bluebird has a light blue back and breast and a white belly. Female bluebirds are brownish but show blue in the wings. The song of the bluebird is a pretty whistle. The eastern bluebird has become very rare in recent years. Scientists think that the use of pesticides and the introduction of the starling from Europe caused the decline in the number of bluebirds. *See also* STARLING. S.R.G./L.S.

BLUE JAY The blue jay is a bird that belongs to the crow family, Corvidae. It is found in central and eastern North America. The blue jay grows to a length of 10 in. [25 cm]. It has a grayish white belly and blue back. The call of the blue jay is a loud "jay, jay." Although its song is not very musical, the blue jay has many calls and can imitate the songs of many other birds. Blue jays flock together and can be very noisy. *See also* BIRD. S.R.G./L.S.

BLUE WHALE The blue whale (*Balaenoptera musculus*) is the largest animal now living on earth. This sea mammal may reach a length of 100 ft. [30 m] and a weight of 150 tons [136 metric tons]. (*See* MAMMAL.) A type of baleen, or toothless, whale, the blue whale has a mouth containing bony plates to strain small organisms from the water. (*See* KRILL.)

The blue whale is a dull blue color. Blue whales live mostly in the colder oceans, near the Arctic and Antarctic regions. During the winter months, the blue whale herds swim to warmer waters near the equator to give birth to their calves. Because blue whales have been hunted for years, they are close to becoming extinct. In an attempt to prevent this, international agreements have been made to limit whaling. *See also* EXTINCTION; WHALE. A.J.C./J.J.M.

BOA (bō′ə) The boas are among the most primitive living snakes. They are nonpoisonous. Most boas live in tropical Central and

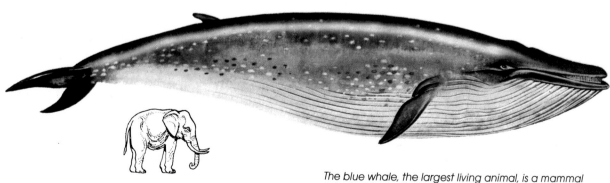

The blue whale, the largest living animal, is a mammal adapted for life in the sea. This drawing compares its size with an elephant's.

Boas, like the emerald tree boa above, are large, nonpoisonous snakes. Boas kill their prey by wrapping themselves around the prey until the victim suffocates.

South America. The largest may be 18 ft. [5.5 m] long. The two species that live in the southwestern United States are smaller, about 3.3 ft. [1 m] long. The boa does not lay eggs. It is ovoviviparous and gives birth to live baby snakes. (*See* REPRODUCTION.) A boa may produce as many as fifty young in each yearly brood (group).

The most famous of the boas is the boa constrictor (*Constrictor constrictor*). Like all boas, it attacks its prey with its long, curved, fanglike teeth. It then coils its body around the prey. As the coils tighten, the prey is unable to breathe, and it finally suffocates. The tips of a boa's jawbones can stretch so far apart that the boa can swallow rodents, birds, and other small animals whole. Its throat and body are also able to stretch. Once the prey has been swallowed, the snake may lie quietly for as long as a week to digest its meal. If upset during this time, the boa may spit out its food. If threatened, the boa becomes active and defends itself. Like all snakes, the boa can go without food for several months at a time. *See also* SNAKE. A.J.C./R.L.L.

BOBCAT The bobcat is a member of the cat family, Felidae. It reaches a length of 3.3 ft. [1 m] and a height of 23 in. [57.5 cm] at the shoulder. The bobcat has reddish brown fur with black spots. The bobcat gets its name because it has a short or "bob" tail. It has twenty-eight pointed teeth and sharp claws on each paw. The teeth and claws of the bobcat are used to kill and eat its food, which is made up mainly of rodents, rabbits, and sometimes deer. Although the bobcat is found all over the United States and Canada, it is now common only in the western part of these countries. *See also* CAT. S.R.G./J.J.M.

BOBOLINK (bäb′ə link′) A bobolink is a bird that makes its home on farmland and in meadows. It belongs to the blackbird family, Icteridae, and can be found in many open parts of the United States. Bobolinks grow to 6 in. [15 cm] in length. The male has a black face, breast, and belly. His back and wings are light yellow, tan, and white. Females are a dull tan color. Males resemble females in winter, at which time the birds live in South America. The bobolink's song is loud and long and sounds like the bird's name. *See also* BIRD; BLACKBIRD. S.R.G./L.S.

BOHR, NIELS (1885-1962) Niels Bohr was a Danish physicist who developed an important theory about the structure of the atom. He based it on an earlier theory by the British physicist, Ernest Rutherford. (*See* RUTHERFORD, ERNEST.) Rutherford had shown that the atom contains a central nucleus. This nucleus is made up of positively charged protons and neutral neutrons. Negatively charged electrons orbit around it. An atom has equal numbers of protons and electrons.

Bohr suggested that when an electron absorbs energy, it then jumps into a wider orbit farther away from the nucleus. He stated that when an electron moves back into lower orbits, which are closer to the nucleus, it gives off energy in the form of radiation. This energy is measured in units called quanta. (*See* QUANTUM THEORY.) Bohr also said that the outermost electrons determine the chemical properties of the atom. He developed his theory for the hydrogen atom, the simplest atom with just one electron. He was able to determine exactly how much energy was involved in each jump of the electron. Bohr was awarded the Nobel Prize for physics in 1922.

During World War II (1939-1945), Bohr served as an adviser on the first atomic bomb project at Los Alamos, New Mexico. He devoted much of his time after 1945 to promoting the peaceful uses of atomic energy. *See also* ATOM; RADIATION. W.R.P./D.G.F.

BOILING AND BOILING POINT Boiling occurs when a liquid is heated so much that it bubbles and changes into a vapor. The boiling point is the temperature at which the liquid boils. At this temperature, the vapor pressure of a liquid is equal to the pressure of the atmosphere on the liquid. At sea level, the atmospheric pressure is 14.7 lb. per sq. in. [1.03 kg per sq. cm], and water boils at 212°F. [100°C]. This standard pressure is called one atmosphere. Above sea level, where the atmospheric pressure is lower, water boils at lower temperatures. At the top of a mountain that is 1.8 mi. [3 km] high, water boils at 194°F. [90°C]. (*See* ATMOSPHERE (UNIT); PRESSURE; VAPOR PRESSURE.)

SOME BOILING POINTS		
	°F.	°C
Acetic acid	224.58	118.1
Aluminum	4,352	2,400
Ammonia	-28.5	-33.6
Benzene	176.2	80.1
Bromine	136.8	58.2
Carbon tetrachloride	170.1	76.7
Chlorine	-29.4	34.1
Chloroform	142.9	61.6
Copper	4,653	2,567
Ethanol	173.1	78.4
Ether (diethyl)	94.3	34.6
Fluorine	-306.2	-187.9
Gold	4,820	2,660
Helium	-452	-268.9
Hydrogen	-432.1	-252.8
Hydrogen chloride	-120.6	-84.8
Iron	5,072	2,800
Lead	3,182	1,750
Magnesium	1,994	1,090
Mercury	678.2	359
Methane	-258.7	-161.5
Nickel	4,950	2,732
Nitrogen	-320.4	-195.8
Oxygen	-297.4	-183
Phosphorus (yellow)	536	280
Platinum	6,872	3,800
Silicon	4,532	2,500
Sodium	1,621.4	883
Sulfur	832.3	444.6
Sulfur dioxide	14	-10
Sulfuric acid	626	330
Tungsten	10,701	5,927
Water	212	100

The boiling point of a liquid stays the same under the same atmospheric pressure. Water always boils at 212°F. [100°C] at sea level, alcohol at 173.3°F. [78.5°C], and mercury at 673.8°F. [356.6°C]. The boiling point of a liquid is usually found by holding a thermometer in the vapor just above the liquid, but not in the liquid. If the atmospheric pressure is increased, the boiling point of the liquid is raised. A pressure of ten atmospheres raises the boiling point of water to 356°F. [180°C]. J.J.A./A.D.

BOLL WEEVIL (bōl wē′vəl) The boll weevil (*Anthonomus grandis*) is a brownish black beetle that feeds inside the seed pods, called *bolls*, of cotton plants. The beetle is about 0.25 in. [6 mm] long. A native of Mexico and Central America, the boll weevil spread into Texas about 1890. Since then, it has spread through most of the cotton fields of the United States. The boll weevil destroys more than 200 million dollars' worth of cotton each year.

The boll weevil, one of the world's most destructive insects, lays its eggs in the seed pods of the cotton plant. The larvae of the boll weevil eat the seeds and cotton. A native of Mexico and Central America, this insect has spread to the cotton-growing regions of the United States.

In the spring, the female lays eggs in the cotton boll. Within a few days, the eggs develop into wormlike larvae, or grubs, that eat and destroy the boll. These grubs become adults within three weeks. Then the process begins again. Several generations of weevils are produced every summer. Pesticides have had little lasting effect on the boll weevil. *See also* METAMORPHOSIS; WEEVIL.   A.J.C./J.R.

BOLLWORM (bōl′wərm′) The bollworm (*Heliothis zea*) is a caterpillar that bores into and destroys cotton plants. It also ruins more than 100 million dollars' worth of corn annually. The adult is a grayish brown moth that lays eggs in the cotton boll, on corn silk, or on other crops. Within a week, these eggs develop into the destructive caterpillars. Bollworms produce two to five broods (groups of young) each year. Tiny wasps are among their greatest enemies. *See also* BUTTERFLY AND MOTH.

A.J.C./J.R.

BONE Bone is a type of hard tissue found in most vertebrate animals. It is one kind of connective tissue. Connective tissue has very few cells and a large amount of a "filler substance" called intercellular matrix. The matrix contains inorganic salts such as compounds of calcium and phosphorus. The matrix also contains collagen, a strong protein produced by the bone cells. Collagen and the inorganic salts are present in bone in roughly equal amounts. The calcium and phosphorous make the bone hard, and the collagen gives it resistance and prevents it from being brittle. (*See* COLLAGEN; CONNECTIVE TISSUE; VERTEBRATE.)

Below is a cross section of the head of the human femur (thighbone). Inside the bone is spongy tissue with marrow in the center.

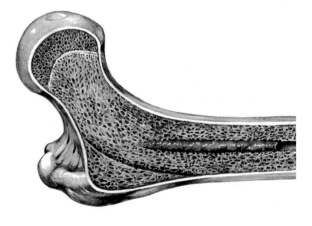

Bone tissue forms individual structures within the body. These structures are called bones. The human body has 206 bones. These bones are connected to form a skeleton. (*See* ANATOMY.) Bones support the body and protect some of its parts, like the brain. Muscles are attached to the bones. Most bones have a hollow center filled with marrow. Blood cells are produced in the marrow and are sent into the circulatory system. (*See* MARROW.)

Bones are formed in a baby before it is born, but they are soft to begin with. After birth, while the baby matures, the bones slowly harden through the process called ossification. The ends of bones remain soft for many years, however, so that the bones can grow longer as the person becomes older. Sometimes growth continues after the bones have hardened. This results in a disease called acromegaly. (*See* ENDOCRINE.)

There are other diseases that can affect bones. Rickets causes children's bones to become soft and deformed. It is caused by a lack of vitamin D and calcium in the diet. Osteoporosis causes bones of elderly people to become porous and brittle. The breaking of a bone is called a fracture. *See also* ARTHRITIS; CARTILAGE; JOINT; LIGAMENT; TENDON.

S.R.G./J.J.F.; M.H.M.

BOOSTER (bü′stər) In space travel, a booster is the first stage of a multistage rocket and is the device that launches the rocket. A multistage rocket consists of two or more sections called stages. Each stage has an engine and a propellant, a combination of chemicals used for fuel. Together, the stages give the rocket enough power to rise into space and travel long distances. As each stage burns up its propellant, it drops away from the rest of the rocket. The booster is the first stage to drop.

After the booster drops, the second stage takes on the task of powering the rocket. To give the rocket the necessary initial speed for space travel, the booster is often much larger than the rest of the rocket. *See also* ROCKET; SPACE TRAVEL; VELOCITY.   P.W./L.W.

BORAGE FAMILY The borage (boȯr′ij) family includes about 1,500 species of dicotyledonous plants that have hairy, rough leaves and stems. This family includes annual and perennial herbaceous plants. (*See* ANNUAL PLANT; DICOTYLEDON; HERBACEOUS PLANT; PERENNIAL PLANT.) The flowers are blue or purple with five petals joined at the base. These plants grow in temperate climates.

The most familiar member of the borage family is the forget-me-not, a blue and yellow flower that grows in most areas of the United

The borage family includes about 1,500 plant species and is found in temperate regions. The family includes the forget-me-not, which is pictured above.

States. The subject of many legends and romantic stories, the forget-me-not has come to be a symbol of friendship and love.

A.J.C./M.H.S.

BORAX (bōr′aks) Borax ($Na_2B_4O_7 \cdot 10H_2O$) is the common name for a soft, white, many-sided crystal that dissolves easily in water. Borax is an important compound of the element boron. (*See* BORON; COMPOUND; CRYSTAL.) The chemical name for borax is sodium borate or sodium tetraborate. The compound is obtained from the minerals kemite and tincal. Most of the world's supply of borax comes from southern California. In one California mine alone, there is estimated to be more than a hundred-year supply of borax. Workers use dynamite to blast loose the solid borax. Large chunks of it are then crushed and dissolved. The solution goes through many steps until borax crystals are obtained.

Borax is used in making glass, soaps, washing powders, water-softening substances, welding flux, food preservatives, enamels, and glazes. The compound is also used as an antiseptic in ointments and eye washes. Chemists use the borax bead test to find out whether substances contain certain metals. A borax bead is made by dipping a small loop of platinum wire into a borax solution. The loop is then heated until a clear, glassy bead forms. Then the loop is touched with the substance to be tested, usually in solution, and heated again. The bead turns a certain color, depending on which metal is in the substance. For example, if cobalt is present, a dark blue bead appears. A light blue bead appears for copper, a brown one for nickel, and an amethyst one for manganese. Borax has also been used in tanning leather and in making paper and textiles.

J.J.A./A.D.

BORON (bōr′on) Boron (B) is a nonmetallic element that appears as a yellowish brown crystal. Boron is found in combination with other elements in minerals such as kernite, tincal, colemanite, and boracite. (*See* CRYSTAL; ELEMENT; MINERAL.)

The United States has large supplies of minerals containing boron compounds. (*See* COMPOUND.) Boron is taken out of these minerals by chemical methods and by electrolysis. (*See* ELECTROLYSIS.) Boron was first isolated in 1808 by Sir Humphry Davy of England. (*See* DAVY, SIR HUMPHRY.) Joseph Louis Gay-Lussac and Louis Thenard obtained pure boron in France in the same year.

Boron is able to absorb neutrons (one kind of atomic particle) without being changed by them. It is used to make control rods for nuclear reactors. (*See* NUCLEAR ENERGY.) These rods control the neutrons that cause atomic nuclei to split. Boron alloys are used to harden steel. (*See* ALLOY.) Compounds such as titanium boride and tungsten boride are heat resistant. They are used in various rocket parts. Useful boron compounds also include boric acid, used in medicine, and borax. (*See* BORAX.) Scientists believe that small amounts of boron aid plant growth. Large amounts, however, are poisonous to plants and animals.

Boron has an atomic number of 5. Its atomic weight is 10.8. It melts at 3,812°F. [2,100°C] and has a boiling point of 4,622°F. [2,550°C]. The relative density of boron is 2.45. *See also* RELATIVE DENSITY. J.J.A./J.R.W.

BOTANY (bot′n ē) Botany is the study of plants. Plants have interested people for thousands of years. The ancient Babylonians and Egyptians observed and named plants. Theophrastus, a pupil of the Greek philosopher Aristotle, wrote *An Inquiry Into Plants* in 300

225

Pollution can cause serious damage to plants. This botanist, a scientist who studies plants, is recording the effects of pollution on the plants in Great Smokey National Park in the eastern United States.

B.C. This was a series of books dealing with the structure of plants. Because of his pioneering work, Theophrastus is often considered the father of botany. The Roman naturalist Pliny included plants in his writings in 50 B.C. At about the same time, the Greek physician Dioscorides listed and described six hundred plants with medical uses.

There was little further progress in botany until the seventeenth century. It was at this time that interest in all fields of science was reawakened. In 1665, the English physicist Roger Hooke observed and named cells in cork. In the 1670s, the English botanist Nehemiah Grew wrote two books on plant structure. In 1735, the Swedish biologist Linnaeus developed a standard way to name and classify plants. (*See* CLASSIFICATION OF LIVING ORGANISMS; LINNAEUS, CAROLUS.) In 1774, the English chemist Joseph Priestley noted that plants give off oxygen in sunlight. (*See* PHOTOSYNTHESIS.) In 1839, the German botanists Matthias Schleiden and Theodor Schwann announced the cell theory. The cell theory states that all living things are made up of cells. (*See* SCHLEIDEN, MATTHIAS JAKOB; SCHWANN, THEODOR.) In the 1830s, the English botanist Robert Brown published a book dealing with the reproduction of plants. In 1865, Gregor Mendel, an Austrian monk, formulated genetic laws on the basis of his experiments in growing peas. (*See* GENETICS; MENDEL, GREGOR.)

All food comes from plants, either directly or indirectly. Therefore, all life depends on plants. In order to understand any living creature, one must first understand plants. The importance of plants has been known since the first crops were sown and the first fields cultivated. Plants have managed to survive and adapt, even to severe climates and to climate changes. Plants produce oxygen and use carbon dioxide, which allows animal life to survive. (*See* CARBON CYCLE; RESPIRATION.) Some plants, such as poison ivy, can be toxic to humans. Still other plants have medical value and can be used to treat various diseases.

Plants are becoming more and more important in today's world. Scientists believe many uses of plants have yet to be discovered. With increased knowledge of botany, there will not only be greater control over plants, but also greater understanding of how humankind fits into the natural world. *See also* AGRICULTURE; ECOLOGY; FOOD CHAIN; HORTICULTURE; PLANT KINGDOM. A.J.C./M.H.S.

BOTULISM (bäch′ə liz′əm) Botulism is a disease of the nervous system caused by a toxin, or poison. The toxin is produced by *Clostridium botulinum*, a type of bacterium. *Clostridium botulinum* produces spores, which can also make the toxin. (*See* SPORE.) These spores can survive the temperature of boiling water, 212°F. [100°C], for hours.

The spores can live in improperly canned foods. If the canned foods contain no oxygen, the spores may give off botulinus toxin, one of the most dangerous poisons known. The human intestine absorbs this toxin and carries it to neuromuscular junctions, the sites where nerves transmit messages to muscles. There, the toxin interferes with the ability of the nerves to tell the muscles to contract. This causes paralysis, a condition where the muscles stop working. People who ingest botulinum toxin may die of suffocation, as the muscles used in breathing are paralyzed. Surgeons may cut an emergency air passage into the windpipe and use a respirator to aid the victim in breathing. Usually, if a person survives the paralysis, he or she recovers completely. If discovered at an early stage, the chances of surviving are much better. The person may take antitoxin to neutralize the toxin in the body.

Home-canned goods are usually the chief source of botulism. Modern commercial canning methods have made botulism rare in the United States. *See also* POISON; TOXIN.

J.J.A./J.J.F.; M.H.M.

BOUGAINVILLEA (bŭg′ən vil′yə) *Bougainvillea* is a genus of about thirty flowering shrubs and climbing plants. They grow in warm and tropical climates. The flowers, in groups of three, are enclosed by three large, bright purple or red leaves called bracts. The leaves are on alternate sides of the stem. Bougainvilleas are showy plants that can be raised from stem cuttings.

A.J.C./M.H.S.

BOWERBIRD (baŭ′ər bərd) The bowerbird belongs to the family Ptilonorhynchidae. It is found in Australia, New Guinea, and neighboring islands. The bowerbird is usually blue-black. It feeds chiefly on fruit. It is named for the fancy bower, or shelter, that the male builds to attract females. The male attracts the female to his bower by placing brightly colored feathers and shells inside it and just outside the entrance. Then he dances and bows before her. Each species builds a different type of bower and uses different decorations and displays. If mating occurs, the

Bowerbirds, found in Australia and New Guinea, are named for the elaborate bowers, or shelters, built by the males to court the females. The bowers are generally made of twigs and decorated with colorful objects to attract the females.

female flies off to build her own nest, a much simpler structure than the male's bower. There, she rears her young alone. *See also* BIRD.

W.R.P./L.S.

BOWFIN (bō′fin′) The bowfin is a very primitive freshwater fish belonging to the family Amiidae. Fossils of this fish hav been found embedded in rocks of the Tertiary period, which began 65 million years ago and ended 2 million years ago. The bowfin is found in more than one-third of the eastern United States and in portions of eastern Canada. It has a long, deep body that can reach a length of 34 in. [87 cm] and a weight of 15 lb. [6.8 kg]. Bowfins live in swampy, weedy lakes and rivers. The bowfin is one of the few fishes able to breathe air. When the water in which the

The bowfin is a primitive fish found in rivers and lakes in eastern North America. It is one of the few fishes able to breathe air.

bowfin is living becomes polluted and there is little oxygen left, the bowfin rises to the surface and gulps air. This air enters the swim bladder, where oxygen is absorbed into the blood. Because of this ability, the bowfin is able to live in water where other fishes cannot. Bowfins eat popular sport fishes and are therefore considered pests by some people. *See also* FISH.

S.R.G./M.J.C.; E.C.M.

BOX ELDER The box elder (*Acer negundo*) is a tree that belongs to the maple family. It is found in many parts of North America. Box

elders do not live very long. They grow to heights of 70 ft. [21 m]. The trunk can be up to 10 ft. [3 m] across. The bark has large, vertical cracks. The leaves of the box elder are different from those of the sugar maple. They have a simpler form, with leaf stalks containing three to seven leaflets. (*See* LEAF.) Although branches of box elder break easily and the tree is often poorly formed, the box elder is a popular shade tree. The wood of the box elder is soft. It is used for making furniture, boxes, and wooden utensils. *See also* MAPLE FAMILY.

W.R.P./M.H.S.

Robert Boyle

BOYLE, ROBERT (1627-1691) Robert Boyle was an Irish chemist and physicist who studied the compression and expansion of air and gases. He is best known for a law he formulated called Boyle's law. (*See* BOYLE'S LAW.) Boyle was the first scientist to believe that all chemical substances exist as either elements or compounds (combinations of elements). He also supported experimentation and the rapid publication of results. Boyle improved the air pump. He studied the boiling and freezing of liquids at reduced pressures.

W.R.P./D.G.F.

BOYLE'S LAW Boyle's law shows how the pressure and volume of a gas are related. It was discovered in 1662 by Robert Boyle, an Irish scientist. The law says that if the volume of a given mass of gas is doubled, the pressure is halved. The reverse is also true. If the pressure on a given mass of gas is halved, the gas will occupy twice the volume. The temperature of the gas has to remain the same for this to be true. The volume of the gas is said to be inversely proportional to the pressure. *See also* BOYLE, ROBERT; CHARLES'S LAW; GAS.

M.E./J.T.; E.D.W.

BRACHIOPOD (brā′kē ə päd′) The brachiopods are a phylum of about 260 kinds of tongue-shaped, marine invertebrates. (*See* INVERTEBRATE.) Also called lamp shells because of their resemblance to old Roman oil lamps, brachiopods are animals with two shells, like bivalve mollusks. (*See* BIVALVE.) One shell covers the top side. The other shell covers the bottom side. Two coiled arms, called brachia, help these animals guide food into their mouths. Brachiopods anchor themselves to the bottom of the ocean by means of stalks, called pedicles, at the rear ends of their bodies. Shells range from 0.2 to 3 in. [5 to 80 mm] in length. Brachiopods are found in all the oceans.

Brachiopods first appeared millions of years ago. They were very abundant during the Paleozoic era (570 million to 225 million years ago) but have greatly declined since then. Geologists have discovered nearly 30,000 species of fossil brachiopods.

G.M.B./C.S.H.

Brachiopods are two-shelled marine invertebrates. Although found in all the world's oceans today, they were more abundant millions of years ago. The picture shows brachiopod fossils.

BRAGG FAMILY One of the most remarkable father-and-son science teams of the twentieth century was that of Sir William Henry Bragg (1862-1942) and his son, Sir William Lawrence Bragg (1890-1971). Working together as research physicists, they studied the structure of crystals by means of X rays. They are considered the founders of solid-state physics, a field that pioneered the development of transistors. (*See* SOLID-STATE PHYSICS.) In 1915, they won the Nobel Prize for physics.

The Braggs developed the X-ray spectrometer. Using this instrument, they discovered much about the atom and how atoms are arranged in crystals. In the same year, the younger Bragg established Bragg's law of X-ray diffraction, a basic rule for learning the structure of a crystal. (*See* CRYSTAL; X-RAY DIFFRACTION.) Sir William Henry Bragg established a school of crystallographic research at University College in London, England. His son founded a school for research in physics of metals, alloys (mixtures of metals), and silicates (minerals that contain silicon, oxygen, and metallic elements) at Manchester, England.   G.M.B./D.G.F.

BRAHE, TYCHO (1546-1601) Tycho Brahe was a Danish astronomer. He made and recorded the most accurate observations possible before the invention of the telescope. Unlike all the astronomers before his time, Brahe observed the planets night after night, not just at certain times of the year. In 1572, Brahe observed a star in the constellation Cassiopeia that had never before been noticed. His observation of this star was the first recorded discovery of a "new" star. It challenged the ancient idea that the heavens could not change. Brahe was also the first astronomer to understand the effect of refraction by the atmosphere on astronomical observations. (*See* REFRACTION OF LIGHT.)

A major part of Brahe's work was the correction of the observations of earlier astronomers. During his more than twenty years of observations in Denmark, Brahe recorded valuable information on many stars, the planets, the moon, and the comet of 1577. His astronomical instruments were kept as accurate as possible. His careful records became the bases of later advances in astronomy. Johannes Kepler, who was his assistant, later used Brahe's calculations to prove that the planets of our solar system orbit the sun. Brahe had believed that the sun orbited the earth. (*See* KEPLER, JOHANNES.)

Brahe's interest in astronomy began when, as a boy, he witnessed a total eclipse of the sun. Although his family wanted him to become a lawyer, Brahe was drawn to the

Tycho Brahe

study of the sky. In 1563, a year after he completed study of the law, Brahe made his first recorded observation. He watched as Jupiter passed between the earth and Saturn. This was the beginning of his scientific career.

In 1571, Brahe built an observatory at a castle owned by his wealthy uncle. He became so famous for his astronomical work that the king of Denmark, Frederick II, ordered him to give lectures on astronomy. Because Brahe also pleased the king with his astrology, the king gave Brahe the island of Hven. Brahe built two observatories on the island, calling them the Castle of the Sky and the Castle of the Stars. These observatories became the models for construction of later observatories throughout Europe. Brahe left Denmark for Poland in 1597. He spent the rest of his life in Prague, where Kepler worked with him. *See also* ASTROLOGY; ASTRONOMY.   G.M.B./D.G.F.